~Where Hope Lives~

Ali Warren

To Marcy,
much love!. Andrea
12/30/2011

Where Hope Lives

Written by Ali Warren

"The purpose of life is to discover your gift and the meaning of life is to give your gift away."
—David Viscott

The Print Shop
Medina, New York
2010

The Print Shop, Medina, New York

Where Hope Lives

Copyright © 2010, Ali Warren

Cover designed by Renee Lama Graphic Design

ISBN: 978-0-9830654-0-1

Printed in the United States of America

This book is based on the author's memories regarding actual experiences in her life. The opinions expressed within this work are that of the author and not necessarily the opinions of the publishers or any other person(s) mentioned within the book. The names and likenesses of some people have been changed to protect their privacy.

Lyrics on page 72 of this work were taken from HANSON'S song "This Time Around" and the author of this work assumes no ownership for these lyrics. All HANSON lyrics were used with permission from 3CG Records.

Back cover artwork done by Phyllis Kipp.

To my parents Marc and Tracy,
you are the two stable rocks on which I stand

To my sister Julia,
you are my lighthouse on the shore,
always showing me the way

For Paul

who has everything he needs

Contents

Chapter 1

Endless Blue

A flower does not plan ahead to bloom, or worry about when the sun will come out to give it warmth, or when the rain will fall to help it grow. The flower just rests, waiting expectantly for the enfoldment of good it knows will come.

* * *

A man walked onto a train. His frame filled the doorway. At just over six feet tall, his stature alone commanded respect, even though he was utterly unassuming. A simple red and blue plaid shirt fit perfectly to his broad shoulders. Thick white hair sat on his head like a crown. The man's chiseled facial features were reminiscent of a fifties movie star and had been softened by age. His eyes still held the vibrancy of youth. He made his way to the back of the car and sat down in a seat next to the aisle, as if he knew he belonged there. He didn't seem to notice that the set of two seats facing each other were already occupied by me; my brown eyes were focused elsewhere. I was average in every way; brown hair, brown eyes, normal height and weight. I attempted to secure my brown hair in a ponytail behind my head, but in an act of rebellion it struggled to get free. I was too busy looking out the window to acknowledge him.

Blessed with a vivid imagination, I was used to traveling places in my mind. It was usually just to escape the boredom I often felt in life, but this time on the train it was for a very different reason.

The man settled himself into the seat across from me. Reaching into his front shirt pocket, he extracted a black

1

leather glasses case. With long fingers he plucked dark-framed reading glasses and perched them onto his nose. From the same pocket, he pulled out a pen and held it loosely between his fingers. He had only a book with him, no luggage. The book was thick with blank leather covers. There was no title or author's name down the spine. The train creaked, sighed, and began to creep forward. The man crossed one long leg over the other and began to read the handwritten words of the thick book he possessed. As he held the pen thoughtfully to his lips, his lean frame reclined comfortably in the seat. The man read with intensity even though he could recite the story in its entirety, as if pulling the words out of the air.

Finally, I met his eyes. I opened my mouth to question his presence but he looked up at that exact moment and smiled. A gap no wider than a fingernail was present between his front teeth. He looked at me over his glasses and spoke seriously. "Hi, Ali."

I crossed my arms. I glanced around the train and saw all the other seats were empty. Unsure as to who this person was and what he was doing inside my head, I responded cautiously. "Hi."

"You can call me Jim," the man said with a twinkle in his eye.

Hesitantly, I leaned forward and gripped Jim's outstretched hand. His skin was smooth but callused; it reminded me of worn leather. As I leaned into him, a smell enveloped me. It was reminiscent of freshly cut grass and strawberries. To me, he smelled like childhood, like home.

* * *

Back in reality, I began my junior year of high school. About a month into my school year, I rode my bike down to the local fire station.

It was sunny on the day that this story began: the perfect, crisp October morning. The sky was an endless blue and church bells rang out, clear and significant. In the years after, I often thought back to this day and felt as if the universe had been mocking me, as if it had no idea that a dark and foreboding sky would have been more appropriate. I met the firefighters on this day, the group would become one of the most significant in my lifetime. As far as people go, from far away they looked complete, but as I forced my way into their world they began to blur around the edges. On this first day, some of them shook the hand I offered, few looked me in the eye, and none returned my smile. The fire station stood there, confident and sturdy, three bay doors wide. I had passed by the building countless times before and it never held any meaning to me. It was just down the hill from my house, but its place in my life was about to become permanent.

Evan was there, a veteran firefighter whom I knew independent of the fire company. While talking after church a few weeks before, his kind face had not faltered when a sixteen-year-old me looked up at him and asked my single most defining question. Evan's response came in the form of a piece of paper that had the words "Fire Company" at the top. I signed my name trustingly and took the first step down the road I was always meant to travel on.

Chief Ray hovered near me as I made my way around the fire station. He stood off in the shadows and eavesdropped on my conversations. His dark eyes watched me attempt to interact with the others, and I noticed him smirk when they did not talk back. It turned out to be Ray who gave me the opportunity to take my first step on that first day.

It was the fire company's annual open house. A makeshift shed stood in the fire company parking lot. Members of the community sat in their lawn chairs to watch the demonstration. The firefighters planned to set a controlled fire on the inside of the shed and show the public how they would extinguish it. Knowing that I was interested in joining the fire company, Ray walked over and explained it all to me.

"We will give you gear." Ray stepped back to glance at my body. "It will probably be big. But it could work if you want to try. One of our assistant chiefs will go in with you and explain everything."

I tried to keep up. "Assistant chief?"

"I am the chief of this fire company. There are four assistant chiefs under me who are in charge of the fire call if I am not there."

As he spoke to me, I was thinking there was no way I could ever do that. I was not a *firefighter* or anything resembling one. How would I know how to put out a fire? But as Ray finished speaking and waited for my answer, I heard myself say, "Yeah, alright."

Under the instruction of a firefighter, I stepped into the gear. A gold badge bearing his last name shone brightly on his chest. The pockets of the giant coat hung down by my knees and the elbows sagged near my forearms. I stepped into the heavy pants. I pulled the suspenders over my shoulders and felt the weight pulling on my hips. The firefighter helped me into the coat and zipped it shut. He picked up the face piece off the ground.

"This goes over your face. The netting goes over your head and the straps pull tight around your jaw."

He pulled it over my head. I moved my hands over the plastic face piece and felt the way it formed to fit me. My mouth was encased in black plastic, with an opening so I could breathe. The air regulator hooked up to the hole. It pressed tight against my cheeks. Someone next to me handed over a black helmet. I smiled at this man, but he did not look in my eyes. I looked at him as he turned his back, wondering what I had done to make that angry look come across his face. I listened intently as the firefighter explained the way to hold the hose.

"Keep it tight to your side so you can maneuver it, but don't hold it too tight. Hold the nozzle firmly, especially when you open it. The force of the water coming out can knock you over. Stay low to the ground and stay as far away from the fire as you can."

The firefighter explained to me how the fire would be burning, and what I should expect when I got inside. I listened to him as I watched the smoke that was beginning to escape from the roof of the shed. He placed the air pack on my back and I steadied myself against the weight. The firefighter told me he was going to hook up the air regulator to my face, and that I needed to take a deep breath for the air to start flowing from the cylinder. He told me that I needed to do my best to breathe slowly so I wouldn't run out of the air supply. I began to sway, to get my body used to carrying all that extra weight. I picked up my feet and set them back down like I was walking in place. I watched the firefighters walk around the shed, watched them get the hose ready and charge it full of water. In all of the gear, I felt like I disappeared.

Then the heavy hose was placed into my hands. I looked down at the piece of equipment I held. A firefighter took the hose behind me and we began to walk, me propelled by his momentum. Under his instruction, I crouched down in front of the closed door. The firefighter opened the hose and water sprayed out. He opened the door and showed me how to control the hose stream by turning the front of the nozzle. I put out the fire I could see while on my knees outside. As a team, we crawled forward and put out the remaining fire in the hay bale. We stood up, turned around and walked outside. The firefighters surrounded me and began to take the gear off. I smiled at one as he reached up and disconnected my face piece. I looked innocently in his eyes and asked, "Can I do that again?"

I turned and walked back into the fire station. Chief Ray was standing there, shaking my dad's hand with security. Ray's eyes were fixed on my father's face.

"I will take care of her, Marc. I promise."

That was all I needed to begin. Tuesday night became fire house night and nothing else mattered except finding my way into this new world. I loved the feeling of my new fire pager hanging on my waist. I was given fire gear: boots, pants, a flash hood, and gloves, all fire resistant. The flash hood went over my face, leaving just enough room for the face mask of the air pack to fit. The bright red helmet made me top heavy and the pants forced me to stand tall as I walked.

I began practicing how to walk and move with the extra weight of the fire gear that pulled my body down. I spent time looking at the new red helmet which signified that I was a junior firefighter. I would get a black one when I turned eighteen and passed certain firefighting tests. I mentally began counting down the days until that milestone. I walked in circles around the fire trucks for dizzying lengths of time, memorizing what was in each compartment. There were power tools and hand tools of every size and shape, each with its own unique job. Each piece of information that I discovered, I made myself memorize. I bought books from the Internet to learn more about the job. I learned that fire engines carry the water and hook up the fire hydrants. Fire trucks have the long ladders that extend up to the roofs of buildings. Rescue trucks respond to car accidents. They have the Jaws of Life on them among many other rescue tools.

I practiced doing jumping jacks while wearing my gear, trying to get used to it weighing down my body. Since no one seemed very interested in helping me get accustomed to my new job, I began to study the other firefighters. I spent my days in anticipation of that first fire call, when I would drop everything and run. When the dispatch center receives a call, a set of beeps or tones come across the pager the firefighters wear. This tells us to get to the fire house to respond.

There are usually more firefighters trying to get to the call than there are available seats in the trucks, so you have to get to the station as fast as possible. Based on listening to the other firefighters, I made this list of what to do when a call comes across my pager:

- Grab keys, sweatshirt, and shoes (not flip flops, because they are not easy to run in and when the tones drop, trust me, you do not walk)
- Drive to the fire house
- Put keys, cell phone, and pager in front sweatshirt pocket
- Go into the fire house
- Once standing in front of gear locker, pull out pants, pull red suspenders to outside of boots, step in, pull over shoulders
- Grab helmet and coat
- Find nearest chief or assistant chief and ask if there is room to ride in one of the vehicles
- Get on the fire truck and fasten seat belt
- Put firefighter ID tag on the ring so people know which piece each firefighter rode on
- Put on headset to hear the dispatcher's voice relaying the call information
- When arriving on the scene, do not open the door until the fire truck has come to a complete stop and the hiss of the air brakes is heard

When one arrives on an accident scene as a firefighter, he or she must determine the answer to three possibly complicated questions. Who needs what, how fast do they need it, and will they die without it? If the answer to the last question is yes, a helicopter is called to fly to the scene and the firefighters find the closest open space for it to land in. That place could be a playground, a field, or the middle of a busy highway. These decisions need to be made within seconds of arriving on scene or lives can be lost.

What the patient or patients need could be anything from a Band-Aid to a hole in their side plugged with gauze. Some people in the emergency services will not hold patients' hands, thinking that it somehow lessens them, I think. Firefighters need to treat people, not just their physical injuries. If what that person needs is comfort, comfort is what they should get. Sometimes all that is needed is a hand held, or a strong shoulder to hold on to, or a tear wiped away. Sometimes when firefighters arrive on the scene of an accident, there is nothing anyone can do. Sometimes it is not about saving people, but about giving them peace when they die.

* * *

The inevitable finally happened. I got my first fire call. It was the night before Thanksgiving when the pager began to beep. My dad drove me down to the fire station, as I was sixteen and could not drive myself yet, as I only had my learner's permit. I ran into the fire station, wide eyed and eager. I waited for one of the firefighters to help me, to tell me what to do.

After a few seconds of being ignored, I followed what the others were doing and I unsystematically put on my gear. I stepped into the fire boots, almost falling over. I caught myself on the wooden wall of my locker as a firefighter ran past me. I called after him but he had already disappeared onto the truck. Pulling my hair into a ponytail, I forced my other foot into the boot and threw the coat over my shoulder. I grabbed the helmet that now belonged to me and began to run too.

The heavy pants weighed me down and made me move with a wider stance. The suspenders were too big, so as I was hurrying to the trucks with my coat in one hand, I was holding my pants up with the other. I still had no idea where we were going, or what kind of emergency had occurred. I clumsily climbed into the engine that had rumbled to life as a firefighter vaulted in on the other side. I sat between two huge firefighters. My small body was almost crushed between their massive arms.

I kept waiting for one of the firefighters staring at me to offer some guidance. I was still waiting for the helping hand to come, to show me how to situate myself in the truck, to tell me how to position the headset so I could hear the dispatcher and the firefighters talking at the same time. I poked the firefighter to my left in the shoulder and marveled at how solid it felt. He pulled off his headset, as if I had already annoyed him. "What happened?" I screamed to be heard over the shrill wail of the siren.

"Wreck on the highway, trauma code." He spoke in fragments and I nodded as if I knew what that meant. Snow began to fall as we sped off into the night to provide help. I could see the snowy trees illuminated by the light the emergency vehicles provided.

The rescue suddenly screeched to a halt. Firefighters climbed over my legs to get out of the truck. No one told me to follow, but I did anyway. I stood in the highway, trying to pull the coat collar up over my ears. Frigid wind whipped around us. The rescue was already parked diagonally across the road, effectively blocking traffic. The firefighters scurried around me, back and forth between the shiny rescue and the mangled cars in front of me. They shouted to each other over the whine of the fire truck's engine. Arms appeared from all directions around me as the rescue truck's compartment doors were yanked open and blankets and tools were pulled out. I tried to take in the scene in front of me.

The driver of the rescue stood next to its massive frame with the control panel in his hands. His gloved fingers grazed each button until he came to the right one. Three immense light towers extended from the roof like mechanical hands reaching toward God. My eyes gleamed in the bright light as they were powered up and shone down, like spotlights from heaven on everyone furiously working. All the firefighters were rushing around, walking fast but not running. I slumped against the warm side of the fire truck, not knowing what else to do. I saw a group of the men with their arms inside the back passenger door of one of the cars. Someone walked past me and suggested that I start to clean up the roadway.

I walked over to the car with a broom in hand. The right passenger side had taken the most impact; the door was completely caved in. It was a distorted mess of black and metal; the door looked like it had been put through a trash compactor. The hub cap on the rear right wheel was cracked and bent upwards. Every piece of metal that was facing the sky was covered with a light coating of snow. I noticed handprints in the snow on the roof of the car, as if people had used it for support when retrieving something from inside. I saw something dark and wet on the ground near the smashed door. Along with broken glass, I quickly swept it under the car.

A stretcher was wheeled into my sight line, being pushed toward a waiting ambulance. There was a little girl on that stretcher, no more than five years old. She was so small that I almost missed her among all the white blankets that illuminated her against the night. She had corn rows in her black hair and the blood on her face was almost concealed by her dark skin. Firefighters moved around the child purposefully, pushing on her chest. Their coats flapped open in the icy wind but they did not notice. Their faces were flushed with exertion. At first I didn't understand why the little girl was lying so still. I didn't understand what exactly was making that look come across the firefighters' faces. For me, there had never been any reason to prepare for something like this.

Most people don't understand what it feels like to watch someone die. It does not always happen in a hospital bed with family and friends gathered around as their beloved takes their last breath. Children do not always outlive their parents. Death is bloody, shocking, and life altering for those who survive.

Rubber-gloved hands came out of the ambulance and lifted the stretcher inside. "Oh God," I said. It wasn't an exclamation but a prayer, said with the deepest longing for a presence bigger than all of us.

That was the moment when it all started. When I saw the little girl's face, the image was captured in my mind forever. I realized that if I trained and learned how to do this job, I could possibly help in a situation like this in the future. That was the moment I fell in love with firefighting. The accident was gruesome, but it was gruesomeness on the face of something pure. That changed it for me. The snow continued to fall silently; it blanketed us and made the world softer. The ambulance sped away and Chief Ray gathered us in front of the engine. I crossed my arms tightly in front of me to ward off the cold. He told us that the fire company hadn't had a bad accident like this in a while, especially one with a child fatality. I nodded at his gaze and felt safe in his presence.

When the firefighters returned to the station, they weren't talking as much as they had been on the way to the call. When I jumped clumsily out of the rescue, I had my helmet in my hand. My brown hair had fallen completely out of my ponytail and the men stared at me.

When I got back home I didn't really know what to do with it all. I stood in front of the living room window and watched the snow continue to fall. I quietly spoke out loud to the snow: "She is not in pain anymore. She is safe and warm and not scared." By that time I was crying, thinking of her face. The little girl was so small and seemed so horribly helpless. The little body that I saw had no more life in it. I

13

wondered how much pain she felt before she died. I wondered if she had seen the other car coming.

In my mind, I escaped to the train. Jim was sitting across from me again, glasses poised on the tip of his nose. He glanced up from the book he was reading. He held the pen over the page as if he was reading over something he just finished writing down.

"You again?" I was surprised to see him sitting so comfortably in my mind.

Jim spoke firmly. "Tell me about her."

"Who, the little girl? No... she died. What is there left to say?"

Jim looked intently at me. I somberly gazed outside and took notice of the broken town that we were passing through. The train's whistle sounded a dismal greeting, but no one outside was around to hear it.

My emotion was displayed in the town, tired. Shingles had slid off the roofs of the abandoned houses as if they no longer cared to stay where they had been put. The houses had begun to lean toward each other as if they couldn't stand up by themselves. The roofs were almost touching, but the discolored concrete of the foundations stood apart until the day when they would collapse in on themselves. The train passed a desolate parking lot, and then a playground. Swings moved in the rough wind, instead of being propelled by children. The sky was a strained blue, as if the color had drained out of it.

Chapter 2

Beginning Love

"A bird is not defined by being grounded, but by his ability to fly."

William Paul Young, *The Shack*

* * *

In the days and weeks after this first fire call, the firefighters began to push me, to test me, to see where I would draw the line. I would find out later that they made bets after my first call to see how long it would take for me to quit. No one offered to talk to me about the death we had all seen. I dealt with it as best as my sixteen-year-old mind could. I never believed in letting anyone see the doubts I held within myself, so I just pushed any doubts aside.

I learned right away to quietly tuck my hair up into my helmet and make sure I didn't have any earrings on to draw more attention to the fact that I was a girl. The firefighters made loud comments about my body, about how I would look with no clothes on. They conversed about where they could take me: the back of their car, the small tool room off the engine bay. With each comment, I found myself being less and less surprised, but it still shocked me. It astounded these men that I was there. They did not know what to do with a young girl that they could not manipulate. I was part of many conversations that went like this:

Men: Hey girl.

Me: Hi.

Men: How you doing?

Me: Fine.

Men: Wanna come out with us? We're going to Hooters.

Me: No thanks.

Men: You sure? It's going to be fun.

Me: I'm good.

Men: (Pointing) You see that guy over there?

Me: What about him?

Men: He thinks you're cute.

Me: How nice for him.

Men: Would you go out with him?

Me: No.

Men: Awww, come on! Why not? He'd treat you real good.

Every time I walked into a fire house, into a new fire class, into any new situation with a new mix of firefighters, they forced me to re-establish myself. Anytime people didn't know me, they would test me to see where I would make them stop. I was always tempted just to get it over with. *Hold on*, I declared to them silently. *Let's get a few things straight. Yes, I am a girl; you can stop looking. Yes, I can and will do this job the same way you do. No, I will not sleep with you or your friend. Not now, not next week, not ever. And my name is Ali, not "Baby." Let's move on.*

But of course I never gave that speech. Instead, I showed them who I was by not giving in to their constant pestering and harassment. It was the "sleeping with them" part that always seemed to confuse the guys the most. In their minds, why else would I be there? A lot of the time, it did not matter what I said. The men did not listen to me when I told them to stop talking to me that way. But the job is not one of convenience. It is one of steady dedication and if one wants to be in it, they have to be all in. I realized that from the very beginning and immediately put myself all in.

I began to train alone. I wanted to be everything these men were, all the power and heroism in them I now strived to find in myself. Because they would not help me train directly, I studied them. I watched them run to the fire trucks, the pant suspenders slapping at their sides. I listened to the way they talked, the special lingo they used in the fire service world.

"The engine is responding" meant that the fire truck was en route to the call.

"Packing up" meant putting on the air packs so the firefighters would not breathe the possibly toxic fumes present in a fire.

"Working fire" meant that there were actual flames involving the house, building, car, etc. People call 9-1-1 to report working fires all the time but the calls are rarely legitimate. Steam from a dryer vent, smoke from a melting water bottle cap that fell behind a dishwasher or fog from a rain storm are all sights that make people report fires. But those two magic words "working fire" meant that someone credible, like a police officer, was confirming actual flames. Talk about words that really make your heart beat.

Most of the men remained at a distance from me. Whenever I had to perform a new firefighting skill, I wished more than anything that I could try it first in private. I wished I could feel the weight of the ladder on my shoulder before I had to throw it against a wall in front of fifteen people. I wanted to be able to pull a hose line off the top of the engine alone before I had to do in front of the entire fire company. The weight of the hose on my shoulder threatened to collapse me to the floor. I would watch the other firefighters and wait until the majority of them were having conversations, wait until their attention wasn't focused on me and then I would begin. They would pause their conversation, walk over near me and then begin again. No matter where I was or where they were, they always kept one eye on me. The firefighters never wanted to helpfully critique my skills, but rather accusingly mock my inexperience. They would watch me to point out the way my arm shook when I extended the fly on the ladder, or the fact that I had to kick the hydrant wrench to get the top to open.

When there were expectations of me, when I could feel eyes glued to my body watching my every move, I was forced to step out of myself and into a world where no God existed. It was a world where night was constant, where I was never right, where I was always in or causing some kind of trouble. That fire house was a place where I didn't always want to be, but it drew me in magnetically and formed a bond I didn't try to break. There was a reverent relationship growing between me and my calling.

I sat in the meeting room on a Tuesday night. The tables were set around the perimeter of the room so we sat in a big circle facing each other. Our shoulders were covered in the same deep blue t-shirts and I found that I was not listening to Chief Ray read off the monthly call totals. I was looking around the room at each face, each mustache and tattoo, trying to memorize the names. I could not see myself ever leaving this group of people, much less being forced out.

After the meeting, I walked through the fire house with an older firefighter trailing behind me. I walked from my locker, back through the meeting room into the kitchen to the vending machines. He stayed right behind me. As I turned to tell him to back off, he looked at me revoltingly and said, "You should be happy to know that my girlfriend is jealous of you!"

I was confused. "Why would that make me happy?"

The man ran off laughing.

I confided in Chief Ray and asked what I should do. He said something about it just being "human nature." Despite his lack of answer, I trusted the look in his eyes as he talked. I liked the stability of Chief Ray in my new constantly changing environment.

Sometimes I wished there was someone like me who had already done all of this. But then I would think that it was okay that I seemed to be the first because I could set the precedent for the girls to come after me. Every time I was asked a question and answered it correctly, every time I completed a skill properly, I challenged the idea that people think female firefighters are a joke. On that same note, I felt like if I answered the question wrong, I not only embarrassed myself but all other female firefighters to come after me.

* * *

The call comes in through the pagers we wear on our waists. Then we drive to the fire house and get into whichever fire truck is due on the call. We have the length of the fire truck ride to prepare ourselves for whatever the call may be. Other than the muted sound of the siren blaring, the only thing we hear is the dispatcher's voice and the thoughts in our own head. Because white lights ruin night vision, the lights in the cab are red at night. So we sit there shoulder to shoulder, knee to knee, and wait.

Stepping out of the cab onto a fire ground is a major shock to the system. We go from forcing our bodies to sit still to forcing our bodies to go a hundred miles a minute and our minds to go even faster. We smell gasoline, something burning, blood, fear, death. People yell to retrieve backboards, wooden cribbing, medical bags, flashlights, a pry bar, a fire extinguisher. We run and yell and pray and try to remember something we read in a book eight months ago that will tell us exactly how to resolve this emergency.

In the early spring, I was sitting at my kitchen table doing homework when the tones came in for an accident on the busy road that surrounded my neighborhood. It came through as a vehicle accident with a pedestrian struck. At those words, I set the pen I was holding down on the table. Hearing the page, my dad ran into the room. He grabbed car keys from the basket by the door.

"What is it?"

I stood up, trying to comprehend the magnitude of the call. I was slow in my hurry. Deliberately, I placed a black hair tie around my wrist. "Accident."

"Are you going?"

I ran to the door as he opened it for me. "Yeah. Yeah. Let's go."

As my dad was hurriedly driving me down to the station, I heard the on-scene chief reports getting worse and worse. Soon the words "trauma arrest" echoed through the pager I was gripping in my hand. I would never forget what that meant: the person we were all trying so hard to get to was not breathing and had no pulse. If no one got to him and restarted his heart within minutes, he would be dead forever.

"Come on, Dad!" I cried because he didn't seem to be driving fast enough for the urgency of the situation.

"I'm trying to stay under the speed limit, Al."

Arriving at the station, I jumped out of the still-moving car as my dad called, "Be safe!" For a split second, I wondered why I was rushing to witness something with the potential to be so tragic and unforgettable. I ran into the station where everyone was quieter than normal. The firefighters were lost in their own thoughts of what they were anticipating to see.

Since it was an accident, the rescue was first due. I was still in the process of getting dressed en route when we arrived on the scene. I jumped out of the rescue and started moving with everyone else toward the crowd of people on the side of the road. The other firefighters all moved away from me and left me standing alone. Chief Ray came up and stood in front of me. Even though the calendar indicated it was the beginning of spring, snow began to fall around us.

Looking down at me, he stated: "This isn't pretty."

I looked past him to the scene. "Yeah, I know. I heard the page."

Ray held up his hands to slow me down. "Ali. You don't have to go up there if you don't want to. It's up to you. There aren't really any jobs for you to do here." Seeing the determination on my face, he added, "I guess you could set up flares on the road."

I appreciated this, but did not want to seem like I could not take the grisliness of the accident. A police officer raced past me and I followed him slowly. Through the crowd of people, I could see a man lying in front of the guardrail. His legs didn't look right, like they were bent in too many different angles. His head was covered in so much blood I couldn't tell if he was alive or had already left us. The faces of strangers bent down to touch him as they tried to push, pull, or will the life back into him. I imagined the breath from the paramedics' own lungs being exhaled to fill his chest. Everyone was trying to bring the man back to life. I could see the struggle in their faces as they tried everything they had been trained to do to make his heart beat again. I felt a sinking feeling as I looked at his body and knew that no one could survive injuries as extreme as that. I had seen enough, and as I turned back to the fire truck, I saw a woman who was crying desperately.

It's interesting to watch people in times of trauma or high intensity; ones who don't experience it often. Some react slowly, as if moving underwater. Time stops for them. They are speechless, breathless; for the ones left behind are the real victims. There are others who are more aggressive. They fight death and try to pretend that everything they just saw didn't happen. They get tunnel vision and see nothing but a life extinguished; no one but the one who isn't there anymore. Their life becomes separated into before and after.

I saw the paramedics loading the man into the ambulance. I just stood there, between the fire truck and the ambulance as the firefighters who had tried to save him began to walk away, defeated. Blood was everywhere: on their hands, coats, boots and faces. They walked toward me like they weren't even seeing the ground beneath their feet. Again, I wanted to talk to them, to say anything, like "this is unbelievably hard and you did the best you could." But I didn't feel like they knew me well enough so I stayed quiet.

It was then that I saw the bike the man had been riding before he was hit by the car. It was lying in pieces of glass, the back wheel twisted and the tire gone completely. His helmet was there too, bloody and broken. My stomach turned. I walked gradually over to where the man had been lying, as if I were walking on hallowed ground. Bloody rubber gloves were strewn around a nauseating black stain in the dirt. Detectives arrived and began measuring the distance of the skid marks and the amount of tread left on the tires of the van that had killed the man. The driver of the rescue extended the light tower to allow them to work into the night. One detective smiled at me as he walked past, spraying neon green spray paint around where the man had been lying. I pulled my eyes away.

I wanted to remember his face so his life wouldn't be forgotten. But if you hold onto that in this job, each face and each life lost, you will soon forget to appreciate the living.

***

One of the men at the fire house began to frequently talk to me. His name was Jared. At first everything was fine. I appreciated that he was trying to make me feel welcome by including me. Then he began to call me almost every day and he left text messages on my phone, over thirty in two days. He told me "promise me that whatever happens will stay between us." I did not know what he thought I would do with him, but I knew I would do nothing. I was sixteen and he was over thirty. I knew that something was wrong.

I knew that I would never be one of the women who got passed around a fire house from guy to guy. But I had never been in a situation like that before and I did not know how to handle it.

Each time I walked into the fire house, I sincerely hoped that somehow Jared would have forgotten about me. But he was always there, a shadow cast over my sunshine. I couldn't tell my parents because they wouldn't let me go to the station anymore. My parents raised me to know who I was and at sixteen, I did. I knew who I was and would never waver from that but I did not know what to do about Jared. He was making me doubt the integrity of the fire house, and making me uncomfortable just being there.

Jared often pushed the limits at the fire house. When the older members of the fire company would get fed up with him every couple of months, Jared would be suspended for minor offenses. But he was always allowed back and each time he returned, he attacked me with more antagonism than before. I talked to Chief Ray and he understood the pressure that I felt to perform better than the men. He said that as long as I tried my hardest, that would be enough. I looked up at him as he spoke. Ray's deep voice rumbled like a diesel engine and I believed all the words he was saying.

I wanted to be everything they were. I yearned for their strength, bravery and courage. I was in love with the fact that I had an opportunity to make such a difference in this job. But no one like me had entered through those doors before. The men asked me how my life was going, if I had a boyfriend, and I innocently thought that they cared. I believed they had faith in me.

After school one day, I was sitting in the office at the fire station looking at other fire companies' websites. Ray was going to come and help me with some extra training that I wanted to do. I heard the back door at the other side of the station open and close. Heavy footsteps fell. Jared rounded the corner and when he saw me sitting there alone, he smiled.

"Hey, Allllllli." He said, drawing out my name. He took a step and sat on the counter inches away from my body.

"Hey Jared."

"Whatcha doing?"

"Nothing."

"Any good calls?"

Jared noticed me alone and saw his chance. He kept asking mundane questions and the more I answered the closer he moved toward me. I kept scrolling through fire companies' websites, looking at all the recent fire calls on the East Coast. He reached over, placed his arm around the back of my chair, and leaned in. He was positioned so he was looking at the computer screen but his face was so close to mine, I could smell his breath. It enveloped me in a stench that fogged up my mind. I glanced down at our arms side by side. The pale hairs on mine were standing straight up. Jared's arm was massive compared to mine, his muscles flexed and his skin rippled. A sinking feeling came over me when I realized I would never be strong enough to make him stop.

Ray opened the back door and at the sound Jared leapt up like he had been burned. Wordlessly, he walked out of the front door, got in his truck, and drove away. I went out to find Ray and we began the training. I forced the idea of an encounter with Jared out of my mind. Chief Ray taught me about hooking up from the hydrant to the fire engine (a technique we call "hitting the hydrant") and he told me about the importance of efficiency in firefighting.

After the hydrant training, I sat in my bedroom writing down the day's events in my journal. My room was one of the only places I felt safe. I could close the door, shut the blinds, and live in the dark where no one could see my face. I moved to brush stray hairs from my face, and as my arm passed in front of me, I caught a whiff of something. It was faint, but as clear as a memory. Jared's smell lingered on the underside of my wrist. I quickly got undressed and stood in the shower. The soap and scalding water rushed down. It was an attempt to sanitize, to cleanse. Jared had never touched me, but I couldn't get his smell off my skin. In my attempt to rid myself of all impressions of Jared, I washed away my innocence. I would never get it back. Jared took my peace of mind with him when he left that day, something so precious, yet so easy to lose.

A few days later, I walked into the fire house. My eyes scanned the room for Jared. When I saw he wasn't there, I walked over to a group of firefighters standing by the door. I put on a strong face, choosing to believe that these men would be kind to me. I was still holding onto the idolized idea of them that I had in my mind. One of the firefighters looked down at me with a smile on his face like he was going to tell a joke. I smiled back, trying to show my friendliness. Instead of the kind of joke I was expecting, this firefighter asked if it was true that I had tried to sleep with Jared. My mouth dropped wide open, my cheeks flooded with surprised embarrassment.

I sputtered. "No... what? No."

"Well, that's not what Jared told us."

The firefighters around me snickered and stared hard, watching my embarrassed reaction. They saw the way my eyes stared at the floor, avoiding their gaze. They jabbed each other in the ribs like school children telling a joke on the playground. I glanced around at the men. I was waiting for one of them to crack a smile, to show that this was just a sick joke. The smiles never came. They believed Jared and wanted some of me for themselves.

I began to put my firefighting into mental compartments. The job was exhilarating and invigorating for me and I was learning more and more each day. The threat of Jared was in a dark place in my mind where I did not allow myself to go. As long as I kept the two separate and did not let the discomfort with Jared affect how I felt about the other firefighters, I was able to keep my head above the surface. When you love something enough, you love all its parts; the moments of frustration and the moments of sheer completeness that let you know you are on the right track.

* * *

One thing so remarkable about volunteer firefighting is that when a call comes in, everyone drops what they are doing all over town and hurries to make the call. People arrive in cars or trucks, on motorcycles or bicycles. They arrive alone or in groups of two or three. Adrenaline starts flowing as they get dressed amidst the activity of others doing the same. The gear lockers line the perimeter of the station, so after getting dressed they all converge on the fire trucks sitting in the middle of the bay. Sometimes I got my fire coat on before the truck started moving, other times I was fighting with the seat belt and trying to get my coat on at the same time while the truck drove out of the bay.

It all depended on the nature of the call and how many people I was trying to beat for a seat on the first piece out the door. I would have one hand on the seat belt release, one hand on the door handle, waiting to fly out the fire truck door as soon as we arrived. I usually had the seat closest to the door so I was the first to get out. If I didn't move fast enough, I would have hands on my back pushing me out of the way. I was teaching myself to move without second guessing, for my body to decide on one action while my mind was figuring out the next. We were usually assigned jobs on the way to the call so once those air brakes hissed, we all hit the pavement running.

Overcome with excitement, I usually ignored the silver steps beneath the doors that could help me get out of the truck perhaps a bit more gracefully, but the job is not about being graceful. Avoiding collision with each other, the firefighters immediately assumed their respective positions. Some ran to the side of the truck and picked up the hose that sat folded in the engine. Others ran with metal wrenches to find the nearest fire hydrant and make sure water flowed freely out before the hoses were hooked up. A few would try to be heroes and walk into dangerous situations without a thought for anyone but themselves. Along with everything else I learned that firefighting is not for the weak, in any sense of the word. Physical strength is needed but mental strength is where one must be the most powerful.

* * *

On the way back from a multiple-company training one Saturday morning, I buckled myself into the fire engine. Rain fell as the firefighters situated themselves in the seats. I felt content, so very peaceful in my newly found place. Across the cab to my left, a female firefighter unbuckled her seat belt and sat on Jared's lap so they were face to face. I snapped my head to look out the window, instantly uncomfortable. The female firefighter was married and her husband was in the engine behind us. Loud rain fell in front of me, smacking into the window like little bullets of moisture. It fell faster than the speed of the fire engine could erase it, so the world in front of me blurred until it washed away completely. The lap dance continued as the fire truck drove down the street, admirable from the outside, but corrupt within.

I knew that I was automatically linked with some other female firefighters because of gender alone, but I was nothing like them. These were women who were in the fire service for the men, not for the job. They used firefighting as a dating service. They went from fire house to fire house, looking for a guy whom they would inevitably find. That was who I was expected to be. A lot of male firefighters assume women are present in fire houses for that reason and that reason alone and they do not easily accept anything to the contrary. When I realized what I was being compared to, I knew I needed to be as different as I possibly could be.

At the beginning of the summer, the members of the fire company held a disciplinary meeting for Jared and me. A few days before, Jared had threatened me with "I heard what you've been saying about me. If I were you, I'd watch my back." I knew I hadn't said anything mean about him, but I had filed a written formal complaint through the fire company. I didn't feel I could handle it on my own anymore. Chief Ray sat across the table from me. I trusted him to fix this problem. During the meeting, I had to read all the evidence I had to show his sexual harassment. I spoke of his persistent phone calls and pestering. Speaking directly to Ray I said, "It seems like he is now getting other people here to be on his side, to turn against me."

Ray remained silent.

I read some of the text messages from Jared:

"Don't take this wrong, but you looked good today."

"You want to sneak out with me tonight?"

"What does my age matter?"

"Don't take this the wrong way, but you looked hot today."

I read on and on. After I was finished, I looked up and told them that his persistence and comments should not be allowed to continue because a member like him demeans the entire fire company. I told them that no firefighter has a right to make other firefighters feel uncomfortable. Will and Chief Ray nodded in agreement. They asked me all kinds of questions and the looks on their faces told me they were surprised by my conviction.

Other firefighters who had witnessed Jared's harassment were brought in. A firefighter named Ricky, who was constantly in motion, came in and told the committee things that he had heard Jared say about me. I was asked to leave while Ricky spoke and as I stood up he winked at me. It was a pleasant wink, a silent reassurance. I smiled at his humanity.

Jared was suspended from the fire company for thirty days.

My parents are the two most loving and supportive people in the world. But these stressful events quickly became too much. The conversations about my treatment at the fire house just stressed them out, so I stopped talking about it and kept it to myself.

* * *

For a week in the summer, I had been doing security through the night with the other firefighters. The company was hired to do 24-hour security for the arts festival in town and we needed to make periodic rounds through the art booths to make sure no one tampered with the merchandise. To pass the time, Will and Ricky showed me how to tie knots that I would need to know for firefighting. I loved that they were so willing to share their knowledge with me. I sat there, with the ropes twisting between my fingers, listening to them tell their stories. They spoke of bloody car accidents, of house fires so hot the fire melted the leather of their helmets. I prayed that one day I would get to have those same experiences.

* * *

On a hot summer night, the fire company prepared for search training. We often used an abandoned two story house that the township had given the fire company permission to use. I rode to the house in the engine with one of the assistant chiefs named Sam, and Will, and Evan. Sam's good humor showed as he joked with me, holding up all the equipment that I carried in my pockets. I helped them set up the house for training before the other firefighters arrived.

The older firefighters went first to test out the training. The point of the evening was to refine our search techniques: how firefighters find victims in a building on fire. By the time my turn came, I was buzzing with excitement and not a bit nervous. I loved the idea of searching. I knew my small size would benefit me. A group of firefighters were going to follow the first group around inside to make sure everything went according to the training plan. My partner and I got to our knees as the front door opened. Smoke rolled out into the evening air. I had a search tool in my right hand to help me search places I could not reach. It was beyond dark inside. My flashlight beam illuminated two feet in front of my face and then stopped at the smoke. An unexpected smile crept to my face. Along with the rest of the chiefs, Will stepped in to the house, looking back over his shoulder at me as he disappeared in the smoke. I whispered into my face piece, "Here we go."

We rounded the corner into one of the rooms and I felt my other senses heighten to make up for my lack of sight. I could hear the chief's boots scuff along the floor next to my right arm. I could make out the hiss of the smoke machine as it puffed more smoke into the house. An uncharged hose line had been placed along the floor and we followed this through another room until we found the stairs. I crawled behind my partner and kept smacking his boot to make sure he knew I was still behind him. I knew how important it was to keep in contact with my partner during a real fire.

Sometimes I forgot which direction I was moving in or where I was trying to go, but I always knew that the important thing was to stay focused on the goal. We were to find the victim and get everyone out as fast as possible, with as little injury as possible. My partner and I began to climb the stairs, still on our hands and knees. We sounded the stairs by pounding on them with our fists because in a real fire it is imperative that you know that the stair step can support your weight before you trust your life to it. We got to the top and went to the left. We entered a crawl space that the chiefs had constructed. The crawlspace was narrow and had wires hanging from the ceiling. My partner went through first, so I waited a bit and when I thought he made it through, I stuck my head in. I heard his muffled yelling. His foot was tangled in the wires. I found his foot with my gloved hand, and then found the pair of wire cutters I kept in the right pocket of my fire pants. I cut the wires and freed his foot. He crawled out of the space.

It was my turn to enter the hole. I made sure to keep my body low to avoid the wires. My problem was, I couldn't lift my head up because the back visor of my helmet would hit the air cylinder on my back. In order to see where I was going, I had to turn my head to the side. I Army-crawled, until my elbows were bruised and kept my body low to avoid the wires. It was a strange position and it made my neck tired and sore. After I made my way through the hole, my partner said he needed to take a break. I lay on my stomach on the floor, resting. Will got on his stomach next to me, to talk in case I got claustrophobic from my face piece. He asked if I was okay, and I was. I love that particular feeling of exhaustion. My muscles were burning and I could feel the sweat rolling down my back. I could not see anything except for the multiple pairs of legs standing around me. Sometimes I just shut my eyes because I didn't really see any differently with them open. Just seeing the blurred edges of objects was throwing me off. When we started crawling again, I stopped when I ran into something, someone actually. It was Sam, the assistant chief. Sam leaned down and told me to wait to see how far my partner would go before he realized I wasn't behind him. I sat up on my heels to wait. My partner eventually called for me and we made our way out of the house. We got outside where the heavy summer heat hit us. I dropped to my knees. I took off the coat and drank an entire bottle of water before I stood up again.

I didn't get to know Will until he was randomly chosen to sit on the Disciplinary Committee. He was soft spoken and relied on the quiet confidence that accompanied his many years of experience. Seeing that I was desperate for guidance, Will began to teach me all he knew about firefighting. He always kept an eye on me and defended me when I wasn't there to do it myself. Will filled the vacant position that Chief Ray had left unfilled.

Back at the station, I was getting my gear back in order in my locker. I was trying to figure out if I would be able to get the boots on faster if the toes pointed in or out when Chief Ray came over and stood next to me. He started asking all about the training. I told him how much fun I had and what I learned.

He turned to me. "You really like doing this, don't you?" Ray looked at me like I was a mystery he was trying to solve. I took the opportunity then to tell him about Jared, who had been calling me in the middle of the night even though he had been instructed to never speak to me again. Ray gave a half-hearted promise that he would reprimand him.

Chapter 3

Working Fire!

"You have to meet the thing. You have to do something in your life that is honorable and not cowardly if you are able to live in peace with yourself. For a firefighter, that thing is fire. It has to be faced and defeated so you can prove to yourself that you meet the measure of the job. You have to stay in the fire."

Larry Brown, *On Fire*

* * *

About a year after I joined the fire company, I got my first call for a working fire. There was a barn on fire in the next town and my company was called to respond. I was at an after-school meeting when the tones went and as I drove the distance to the station, I fought to drive under the speed limit. It took me about ten minutes to get to the station so when I pulled into the parking lot, the engine was idling on the front ramp. It had been about thirteen minutes since the original call came in. I flew out of my car and immediately disappointed when I realized that since I was not yet eighteen, I was not allowed to ride in that particular engine. The cab of the engine did not have a roof; it was completely open other than the sides where the equipment was held. The only part of the engine that had a roof was in the front where the driver and officer sat.

A firefighter got mad and yelled to the others. "We need to go now! But we need one more to respond." Without looking at me, he gestured. "Damn it, she can't ride in this piece!"

Will calmly came around the side of the engine. "Ali will sit up front. When we get to the scene, I will be the officer and she will be a part of the crew. Let's go. Now."

It is a common and well-known rule that the person who sits up front in a fire truck is the highest-ranked person going on the call. They are the one who calls the shots for the rest of the firefighters. So on an ordinary call, I did not have enough experience to ride in that seat. But Will made an exception in order for us to have enough firefighters to finally respond on the call.

I was thrilled to be able to sit up front for my first working fire. One of the assistant chiefs climbed into the driver's seat. A crew of three was in the back. With me up front, the engine was full and they could now respond. I thought about the things I had been watching the other firefighters do when they were in the officer's position. I needed to sign the engine on to the dispatcher, telling them that we were finally responding. I was tingling with excitement and reached across to pick up the radio. In my head I said "County, engine is responding." As I held the radio to my lips and put my finger on the button to talk, the firefighter driving took it out of my hand and signed the engine on himself. I was confused because the driver's only job is to drive. My hand hovered in the air like it was still holding the radio. My instinct was to call him on it, but those thoughts were quickly forgotten because I was going to a fire!

As we drove, a black cloud appeared in the sky. I could imagine the burning barn at the other end, like a pot of gold at the end of a rainbow. We turned down a side street and passed an engine pumping water from a creek. Rounding the corner, I caught sight of the fire. A barn was rapidly burning; long flames licked and hissed at the wood it was trying to consume. I was mesmerized by its power. I had never seen that much fire before. As we stepped out of the truck, the wind shifted and radiant heat made me take a few steps back and turn my face away. Weak from the heat, the tin sheets on the roof began to collapse. The smoke mixed with steam from the fire hoses and drifted up into the vibrant bright blue sky, changing its color to gray.

When a working barn fire is announced over fire dispatch, the firefighters responding know that it will probably be burned to the ground by the time the water gets there. Since barns are made of wood and contain hay and very flammable material, they burn hot and quickly. Not a lot can be done to save them. We simply watched it burn and made sure the house near it was in no danger of catching on fire too. After the barn finished burning, we began to clean up. I stood on a piece of burnt metal with a long metal tool in my hands. We moved the scraps of metal and charred timber around, looking for hidden pockets of fire that was still burning. The firefighters' gloved hands gripped the hose with confidence as they walked through the debris. The letters on the backs of their jackets looked like they were melting as the heat came up behind them in waves.

The next night during the fire training at the station, a screaming match took place. It was all about me. A few minutes before at the fire company meeting, Ricky made it clear that he was not okay with the fact that I went on the barn fire. He wasn't even on the call, but was doing the speaking for another firefighter who was. My perception of Ricky changed instantly and forever. I tried to catch his eye for some sort of an explanation, but he wouldn't look at me. He would never again look me in the eye, not once.

After I left in the engine on the barn fire call and the firefighters didn't hear my voice come over fire dispatch, they believed it was because I didn't know what to do. They said that there was no way I belonged on a fire truck if I couldn't even manage to work the radio. No one told them the truth.

There was brief talk of disciplinary action against me for being so "incompetent" and against Will for making the decision to let me go on the call in the first place. After the meeting, everyone filtered out into the truck bay. They all started talking about me, not even caring that I was within ear shot. Chief Ray was in the lounge making copies and motioned to me as I walked by. He closed the door behind me.

"Look at me." Ray said firmly.

I did.

"Don't get mad. Go out there and act the way you always do toward them. Be no different. This will be okay."

I nodded quickly.

As I walked out of the truck bay just a little reassured, I saw Ricky walk into the truck bay out of the corner of my eye. He walked directly over to Will and began to yell. The next thing I knew, they were toe to toe, yelling into each other's faces. My eyes darted back and forth between them as my heart raced. Chief Ray swiftly marched over to them, and Ricky began yelling at him. I could not believe he had such little respect for his fire chief.

When my mom picked me up from the station, all the tears I had been holding in fell out and I cried all the way home. My mom held me like she was trying to hold the pieces of my heart together.

Troubled, I lay in bed that night looking into the dark. I whispered a newly found question that at the time had no answer.

Jim slid into my mind and spoke without me needing to prompt him.

"When you have a dream, it's yours. It's not your friends' or your parents' or society's or the world's. It's yours and you choose what you do with it. Nothing can take it away or change it unless you let that happen. Most dreams naturally evolve over time as the dreamer matures. The overall goal stays the same, but the process by which to bring it about falls away and grows back differently, unexpected but perfect."

I took Jim's words to heart and they comforted me. I lay there at a crossroad. My decision affected no one but me, no life but this one. I also understood that because of who I was and who I would not be, this would never get easier. In that moment, I accepted the weight of the world. It fit into my heart perfectly. I had to convince myself every week to go back to the fire house after the way I had been treated. But each Tuesday night, the lines I had drawn between the bad and the good began to blur. What new rumor will the men start this week? What will they ask me to do to make me fail in front of them? How many more people will turn against me? I wanted so badly to not fail in front of them.

My back was starting to hurt from all the weight on my shoulders. I just wanted to get through the next Tuesday night training in one piece. But I knew even if I did that, there would always be another one looming over me. There would always be another Tuesday night, another test. The one and only comforting thought that kept me going was this: I knew that by me being there and being myself, I was shattering every degrading thought those men had about female firefighters and our place in the world.

Jim's voice filtered in and out of my mind. Sometimes at night I was still alert enough to hear it. Other times his face appeared in my dreams. One night long after everyone else had fallen asleep, I lay awake and listened to the rain. I tried to make sense of the world and the fact that I felt forced to become someone who I did not know. I listened to the rain pounding on the roof above me, a heavy rhythm, which eventually beat me to sleep.

* * *

A few nights later around 4 a.m., a call came in for a building fire. Since I was still under eighteen, I was not allowed to go on calls after midnight on school nights because of child labor laws. But as soon as the tones went, I was wide awake and my body wanted to be doing something, so I got out of bed and plugged in my scanner. A scanner is like the pagers firefighters wear on their waists, but instead of only picking up the main firefighting channel, it picks up all the police and fire ground channels for the entire county. This way, firefighters can hear all the action during a fire call. I crawled back in bed and found the fire ground channel that the call was operating on. Cradling it in my hand, I lay there in the dark and listened. I began to quiz myself like I usually did, listening to the chief's reports and seeing if I could figure out what they were going to do before someone talked and gave it all away. I listened to their strong, calm, excited voices and like a lullaby, they carried me to sleep.

* * *

Jared's thirty-day suspension was over. While he was gone, I heard that he had been pestering people for information to use against me when he came back. It was the storm cloud forming in my idealistic blue sky. I thought to myself, *I need to run a fire call so I can remember why I do this.* Sometimes the foolishness with the firefighters made me forget why I was there. I began to lock certain memories into my mind so I could recall them when it all got to be too negative and too much.

* * *

Different fires have different smells. Bonfires, wood stoves, and house fires each smell differently. Car fires, however, smelled the worst to me—rubber tires, leather

43

seats, and plastic all mixed together in gray smoke so thick that it clogs your lungs. The smell of it clings to your hair even long after you've showered. One night while I was studying for a vocabulary test, tones came in for a working car fire. I went running, forgetting to wear shoes. In the winter, shoes were definitely a must, something easy to slip on and off. But socks were needed too; those rubber fire boots will rub bloody blisters into your heels without them. Hurrying out of my car, I ran up to the station right behind Will, who paused to hold the door open for me. Side by side, we pulled on our gear. We both spoke breathlessly, even though we hadn't even begun to work yet.

"Where?" I asked.

"By the baseball fields. Dispatch said it is fully involved." Will answered.

"Occupants?"

"Not sure."

Side by side, Will and I turned and ran to the fire truck. Since I was still a junior firefighter, I had to wait for permission to get on the fire truck from one of the chiefs.

I was standing between the engine and rescue, jumping from foot to foot with pent-up adrenaline, hoping more than anything that I would get to go. The engine was first due for the fire, and the driver was waiting for one more person to show up to make the crew complete. The dispatchers came over the radio and told them again the call information: location, fully involved car fire, all passengers were out of the vehicle. Then the firefighters in the engine began pounding on the window and when I looked, they motioned for me to get on. That gesture alone brought joy. They needed *me*.

We drove lights and sirens down the road and I felt like my heart was going to burst out of my chest with happiness at the mere sound of it. Will could not find his flash hood (the fire-resistant hood that covers the head and neck of the firefighter) so he asked for mine. I reached into my front pocket and handed it to him, happy I was able to help. The duty chief had made it to the scene and confirmed to us that it was in fact a fully involved working car fire. As we slowed down to approach the scene, I turned around in the seat and was greeted by the sight of flames. As the driver jumped out of the cab, he yelled to me to chalk the wheels of the engine. I knew it was always the driver's job to do that, but I did not argue. As the men rushed at the car with the hose line that sat in the front bumper of the engine, I took the two wheel chalks and set them behind the giant tire. The driver pumped foam through the hose line to more effectively extinguish the gasoline that was on fire.

Since I wasn't going to be actually fighting the fire, I did not need to wear an air pack. With my coat open in the wind, I took a few steps toward the burning car and felt the radiant heat touch my face. The flames ate at the metal furiously and this produced a breeze that lifted up the ends of my hair, making them dance around my face. The burning car sat beneath trees and I watched the leaves flutter as the invisible heat rose up and made them move. The firefighters fought with the hardened hose line. They approached the car from the side and attacked the fire with the hose coming down over their shoulders. The nozzle was opened and white foamy water poured out.

I felt a few pats on my shoulder. I turned and saw a firefighter who had come on the second engine. I had been so mesmerized by the sight of the flames, I hadn't even heard the engine pull up behind me. He was hustling his way to the fire. I felt a few pats on my other shoulder and it was Chief Ray doing the same. He turned around to smile at me and suddenly, I remembered. I remembered why I liked this job that sometimes caused me so much pain. I felt like they were saying, "Hey, it's good to see you, sorry you can't come and play with us."

Will broke out all the windows of the car with a halligan bar. (A halligan bar is a long metal bar with forked ends on one end and a blade and tapered spike on the other. It is used mostly for forcible entry but is also very effective at breaking most anything.) The glass shattered and then glittered in the flashing lights. I could see him moving his arm around inside the car while trying to keep his face out of the smoke and I knew he was doing a sweep of the seats to be absolutely sure there was no one inside.

After a while, the firefighters needed the cylinders on their air packs changed. When I first started firefighting, I sat on the floor of the station with an air pack in my lap and practiced forcing the cylinder in and out, in and out, securing it and loosening it again. Now I could do it in my sleep. As the firefighters walked toward me, I remembered the steps perfectly. The firefighter who took the radio out of my hand on the way to the barn fire wanted his cylinder changed first. His back was to me and the empty air cylinder faced me. I hesitated. I imagined the situation reversed, me waiting for one of them to help me. I briefly toyed with the idea of taking extra long to change the cylinder or lying and telling him I needed to go find another one. I could have delayed him getting back to the smoldering fire and blamed it on an equipment problem. But I changed the bottle as fast as I could and tapped him on the shoulder. He was good to go.

Standing there, I secretly laughed at the path I had chosen. Or rather, the path that had chosen me. I was the girl who wore paper clips as earrings before I was allowed to get my ears pierced. To my parents' fruitless protests, I wore fancy shoes and purses while helping them garden in the summer. I was the girl who made my little sister pretend to be sick when we were young, just so I could take care of her. Now nothing made me happier than riding down the street in a fire truck with lights and sirens going. My greatest fear was always that people would look at me and never give me the chance to be something great. I was afraid of not being allowed to find my place in this world. I was never afraid of the job, for the tragedy I knew I would see, or the life-and-death decisions I knew I would someday have to make. I was afraid of people not giving me the chance I deserved to succeed. I felt like I could get through the difficulty of working with the men because I felt like I could handle it. It was all for that end result.

* * *

Will warned me that things were probably going to get worse, that the firefighters were going to be more bold about purposefully setting me up to fail. The firefighters were running out of ways to make me feel unwelcome.

On the third day of the new year, I was sitting on the floor of the fire house truck bay. The trucks loomed on either side of me, and provided some privacy as I twisted a green rope between my fingers. I was trying to teach myself more knots. Suddenly, I noticed Ray standing in front of me. He was leaning against the back of the engine, his arms crossed. He had been watching me.

"Oh! Hey, Chief."

"Hi. Let's talk in my office."

It was not a question. Leaving the rope in the middle of the floor, I followed him. I could not help but notice the silence that echoed through the station. There was no one else around. Glancing behind me, I walked into the chief's office. Ray shut the door behind us. He gracelessly began to speak.

"I just think you should not force your hand here. Try not to make waves. I just think...I don't know. Maybe you should just take a break? I don't know... if this is right for you."

They were statements formed as questions. Ray was standing over me while I sat in a chair.

"We have never had a sixteen-year-old girl here before." That was his excuse, but not the reason.

"So?"

"It's making us weaker."

"Us, who?"

"The company."

"What? How?"

"You are forcing people here to change."

Ray told me that people believed he would never punish me.

"Punish me for *what*? I didn't do anything!"

But I realized what he was saying. I looked at him fiercely, wanting to challenge him, but I was startled by the presence of hatred in his eyes. I wondered when that seed had been planted. When I realized Ray was trying to talk me out of being a firefighter there, my entire perspective of him changed. I walked out of his office in a kind of a daze. My safety net now had holes.

But the silent struggle continued, a quiet revolution to promote equality for humankind.

Sometimes the thing we need the most is to very simply
know that we are not alone.

Chapter 4

No Limit

"There is only one way one can endure man's inhumanity to man and that is to try, in one's own life, to exemplify man's humanity to man."

Alan Paton, *Cry, the Beloved Country*

* * *

Firefighting is so unpredictable. While frustrating at times, this is one of the qualities that makes it so magnificent. It is not like sports in the way that there is a championship game at a set time in the future that firefighters can train and prepare for. There are no instant replays, no weather delays, no do-overs, no time-outs. All there is is the *moment* and what we do in it can never be changed or taken back. A firefighter's big moment can come at any second of any day. Stepping into the shower: fire call. Out to dinner with the family: fire call. While drifting off to sleep at 11 p.m., while sound asleep at 3a.m.: fire call. In 90-degree heat with 90 percent humidity, in 10-degree blizzard conditions while you have a cold: fire call. Despite its unpredictability, each call demands that firefighters give all of themselves, and hold nothing back. The one thing that firefighters can be sure of is that their one call will come, the one that will define the rest of their days.

On a January night, my fire company was dispatched to a vehicle accident with rollover and ejection. Put into simpler terms, a car had rolled over and one of the passengers had been ejected out of it. I was watching television and had let my mind drift into another world when the tones sounded. I leapt up from where I was sitting. My mom heard the tones from the other room and yelled after me to be careful.

Nothing in the past few seconds mattered, my mind began to prepare myself to respond to this call. Adrenaline began pumping through me because I knew this call had the makings of being something big. From the moment I arrived at the station, I felt like something was different about this call. The feeling was electric. People came into the truck bay from different directions, looking disheveled. I got dressed faster than I ever remembered doing before: boots, pants, coat, helmet, turn, run.

The fire truck driver pressed the gas pedal to the floor and we braced ourselves against each other to stay upright. Hands reached for the boxes of rubber gloves, for the flashlights that charged above our heads. I suddenly became afraid of what I was about to witness. I did not want to observe another death. I didn't feel ready. I would learn that no one is ever ready to witness death and just because you have done it once doesn't make it easier the next time. I focused on pulling my rubber gloves on and making sure they were secured tightly into my coat sleeves. I briefly noticed that my coat didn't seem to make my body disappear anymore. Somehow, I had found my place.

As we pulled up to the scene, I saw the hulking frame of a dark SUV laying on its right side off the roadway. Will and I sat across from each other in the rescue, our hands gripped our knees. We glanced at each other, collectively gathering our courage. The air brakes hissed to a halt. I jumped out of the rescue first with Will right behind me and we both hit the ground running. I took in as much of the accident scene as I could. There was a crowd of people kneeling around someone lying on the ground to the right of the SUV. It didn't seem like anyone else was hurt. Police cars were scattered across the two-lane road, their blue lights reflected in the broken glass that shone across the highway. I grabbed a new blanket out of the rescue and began pulling it out of the plastic as I walked over to the crowd. I knelt down next to a teenage girl and braced myself for the extent of whatever shocking injuries she might have. People had been trying to keep the girl warm in the January night air, so we quickly pulled off all of the sweatshirts and blankets that covered her. I almost looked away, afraid of what I might see, but I saw no broken bones or blood. I laid the blanket over this poor girl who was lying in the dirt and tried to tuck it around her petite frame.

Her hands came out from under the blanket and curled into tight fists. They started waving back and forth and she was shaking out of fear and shock. I looked at her desperately, wondering what I could possibly do to help her. How could I fix this? Firefighters were treating all of the girl's possible injuries, such as a broken neck, concussion, or internal injuries. I don't know what made me do it, but I reached out and grabbed this girl's shaking hand. She squeezed it immediately with a strength born out of fear, the way someone would grab onto a life raft if they were drowning. She held my hand so tightly it probably should have hurt. I began to do for this girl what she could not do for herself.

My eyes rested on a diamond stud in her nose. I suddenly remembered a petite girl with striking blue eyes running around on a soccer field with my sister. This girl's eyes were darting around at the big men that were kneeling and standing around us. I saw those eyes again and a name entered my mind.

"You're Kelly, aren't you?"

Kelly's eyes quickly moved to look at me. "Yeah." Her teeth chattered in between her words, her breath was unsteady. She shook uncontrollably. "Who are you?"

"I'm Ali...Warren. You played soccer with my sister, Julia, in high school. My dad and your dad are in that business group together."

She spoke as if she had just finished running a marathon. "Oh...yeah...I know you. Hi...can you...I have something in my eye."

"Okay, let me see." There were at least a dozen men standing and kneeling around us, but I don't remember them being there. I just remember her.

With controlled steadiness, I reached up and wiped her eyes, rubbing away Kelly's smudged mascara with my rubber-gloved finger. I noticed the dirt and gravel throughout Kelly's light brown hair that must have come from her tumbling across the road. Her other hand was also shaking uncontrollably. Hunching over her, I grabbed it and we became locked together, two as one.

I became a human shock absorber. The tighter Kelly squeezed, the stronger I became to compensate. It was effortless. Kelly's fear became less as it flowed into me and I just let it go. The commotion around us grew as more firefighters arrived on the scene. Kelly's breathing slowed to normal, her eyes locked on mine. I got my face down close to Kelly's, like I was going to tell her a secret. Strands of our hair mixed together and blew around our faces. All Kelly could see was me so she could ignore the commotion of the men around us.

"Good. Good." I said, just loud enough for Kelly to hear. "Just look at me. Just breathe." I was reminding myself to do that too. I knew they needed to fit the backboard underneath Kelly to prepare for the arrival of the ambulance, and as I told her this, Kelly began to cry. Uncontainable tears spilled down her face faster than I could wipe them away. There were no words I could say. I knew we needed to roll her onto her side quickly. The frigid air threatened to steal our breath away. Wearing pounds of extra clothing I was freezing; I couldn't imagine how cold Kelly was. With my body I tried to protect her from the wind and the intrusive lights shining all around us.

With our hands fastened together like they were glued, Kelly's eyes struggled to focus on mine as she was fighting the pain. I looked up and saw the other firefighters' faces. They knew as well as I did that if Kelly couldn't calm down she could make whatever injuries she might have worse. I needed to get her attention so I spoke quickly, but clearly.

"Hey. Hey! Listen to me. Just listen to me, that's all you have to do, just listen to me and we will do the rest. We have to roll you right now, to get you onto the backboard."

One of the firefighters nodded to me and I positioned myself next to Kelly while still holding on. Kelly was rolled toward me, and in one fluid motion the backboard was slid on the ground underneath as her body was held steadily. Her face instantly crunched up in pain and she screamed out, but I confidently yelled to her that it was going to be over soon. The firefighters rolled her onto her back as Kelly gritted her teeth together to keep from screaming. On the count of three, she was lifted into the air and we made our way over the guard rail to the waiting ambulance. I was still holding on tightly and did not plan to let go before she was ready. More people appeared and straps moved around us, tightening Kelly to the stretcher. As Kelly was secured to the stretcher, it released her from me and I didn't feel like I had to protect her anymore.

After they loaded her in, the paramedics stood outside the ambulance to talk to the police officers. I climbed in beside her. Kelly spoke quietly to me, as if she were drifting off to sleep. Her voice wavered as she slid into shock.

"Ali, thank you. Thank you. I don't know how this happened. I thought I was going to..."

I put my hand on her arm. "You're not. You're not. I know that this seems impossible right now, but it's...it's just going to be a good story to tell when it's all over. You are okay now."

As she cried quietly, I held one of her hands in both of mine. A tall paramedic with a shaved head climbed in next to us. Touching two fingers to Kelly's wrist he looked at his watch and counted her pulse.

"Alright girls, we have to go. The ER is expecting us. Firefighter…"

"Warren."

"Firefighter Warren. Your rescue is taking up."

This meant that the rescue truck I rode to the scene in was getting ready to return to the station. "Okay. Thanks. Kelly…"

Kelly squinted her eyes against the bright fluorescent lights of the ambulance. She spoke quietly as the medic covered her with another blanket. "Ali, thank you."

I felt emotion collect in my throat. Tears formed at the corners of my eyes. I glanced at the paramedic, who was looking back at me. Smiling at him, I squeezed Kelly's hands and jumped out of the ambulance. I stood there in the middle of the closed roadway feeling like a part of me was driving away. The ambulance left then, its white box body disappeared into the dip in the road. In that exact moment, as the flashing lights grew dim, I discovered something. I realized, with sudden permanence, that I would give away any part of myself if it would make someone else whole.

Firefighters never know what they're going to find when they step out of a fire truck. We do, however, undoubtedly know that we will find some way to deal with whatever it is. We dig down deep into ourselves and find strength we didn't know we had. If that means hardening our heart for a few moments so it doesn't break while we witness something, we do it. If that means tightly clenching our stomach so we don't throw up, we do it. If that means giving every ounce of strength we possess to someone else, we do it. Our strength doesn't diminish when at a victim's side. We get an intimate look into the person and try to find something for them to connect to that will make them believe they are strong. We do it all. And it doesn't matter what effect it has on us. When we get into that gear, we begin living for a purpose that's greater than ourselves. In those moments that's all that matters. That's it.

I turned back to the firefighters who were sweeping the roadway clean of broken glass, making room for the tow truck to come and flip the car back onto its wheels. I smiled at the faces who never failed to scowl back at me, feeling lightness in my heart. I was oddly at peace that night as I waited for sleep to find me. The feeling I was chasing had eventually met me in the same place. I felt as if a part of my future had fit into my heart. Finally.

After school a few days later, I walked into the kitchen. My parents sat at the table. The phone sat in front of them.

"What's going on?"

My dad smiled proudly. "I talked to Kelly's dad today."

"Oh my God, how is she? Is she okay?"

"She is. She will be. She called you her 'rock.'"

I smiled. The emotion that I had not been able to suppress since the accident came in the form of tears.

***

A building fire occurred in town. The neighboring fire department's rescue was out of service, so my fire company was due to provide theirs. The tones sounded and once again, an ordinary day was interrupted by the extraordinary. The ride to the fire ground was longer than usual, and while we hurried to get downtown, the sight of cars moving to the side of the road was never so incredible to me. The dispatcher came over the radio and announced to all that we indeed did have a working fire in a building that consisted of four townhouses.

As we approached, the fire building became apparent as firefighters were already on the scene. Towering scene lights were haphazardly placed; electrical cords reached out from the engine and ran parallel to the hardened fire hoses. Since my fire company was not needed upon our arrival, Evan asked me if I wanted to take a look around the fire ground. We walked around to all the different fire trucks and saw how they were operating. We saw the different groups of firefighters working together, carrying ladders and flashlights and extra cylinders full of air. Around the back of the building, all the windows were broken out and ladders were firmly placed below them. They were there in case firefighters inside needed to make a quick exit. The front door was open; firefighters were going in and out carrying wet sections of hose, flashlights, and long ceiling hooks, which were used to tear down the wet and ruined ceiling in the apartments. Evan and I passed them on the stairs, and I saw the sweat glisten on their faces.

After most of the action had died down, I was standing in the street observing the fire scene before me, watching firefighters discuss the call. I had a radio clipped to my coat to hear the fire ground communication. A firefighter's voice came over the radio and asked a firefighter from that company to shut the hydrant down. Even though I was capable, since I was under eighteen and could not perform all firefighter functions, I didn't move to do the task. I also saw two older firefighters coming toward me, and I didn't want to take their job. Patrick, whose dark eyes always seemed to follow me around a fire ground, appeared next to me. Patrick was one of those people who never said much, but always seemed to make sure his opinion was known.

"You heard them. Shut it down."

I watched the firefighters walking toward me, hydrant wrench in hand.

"Um...I'll let them do it. It's not our call and they are coming to do it anyway. Look."

I gestured down the block. Without speaking, Patrick walked away. I sighed, knowing that I would have to face the consequences of that later.

* * *

The next day I went on a call to a minor house fire. A mattress had caught fire and filled the small attic with smoke. The fire was out before the firefighters arrived. I learned a few new things on the call, like how to operate a water can. A water can looks like a silver fire extinguisher and it is filled with water. I also learned how to look at the ground and close my ears when firefighters from other companies walked past me because if I kept hearing what they said about me I knew I was going to lose my faith in people.

Calls frequently came in the middle of the night. When they came in on Friday or Saturday nights, I was allowed to respond because there was no school the next day. When I arrived, the men would tell me that my face looked dirty and that I should take a shower before I came next time. They snickered as I struggled to find the words to disagree. Because of this I stopped looking them in the eye and soon, this became easiest.

* * *

I was doing my very best to follow the rules. When one of the firefighters came up with a new rule on the spot, I just added it to the list and kept going. The firefighters saw that Ray was doing nothing to halt their efforts to throw me out, so they were free to treat me as they wished. I was counting up my weekly hours in the Junior Firefighter sign-in book. That was a new one: someone had decided to become obsessive about making sure all my hours were accounted for. I couldn't remember who it was. All of my enemies were beginning to blend together. Not only did I have to account for all my hours in the log book, but I had to be gone from the station by 10 p.m. It didn't matter if the company was doing training or having a meeting, I had to be gone.

I was counting up hours on my fingers when Patrick stormed into my sight line. As soon as I saw him, I knew something was wrong. His face was corrupted with fury. He beckoned at me and like a dog being pulled on a leash, I followed. I found Chief Ray waiting for us in the meeting room and I figured that they wanted to talk to me about something leftover from Jared's suspension. I was still carrying the Junior Firefighter sign-in book in one hand, and a pencil in the other. Still vaguely adding up hours in my head, I wondered how long it was going to take because I wanted to get outside to watch the training going on in the parking lot.

Patrick pulled the door closed behind me. Click. It locked shut. It was just the three of us standing in a triangle, facing each other. Patrick let loose a string of infuriated babble, startling me so much I dropped the book I was holding.

"Why is it so hard for you to just do what you are told?"

All the air got sucked out of the room.

I stared at him, rapidly trying to prepare for what I knew was coming. "Excuse me?"

"You disobeyed a direct order from me by not shutting down that hydrant."

"No, I..."

Patrick patronized me.

"That's known as *insubordination*."

I glanced over his shoulder at the heavy door. It was locked and a code was needed to open it. Patrick's arms loosely swung by his sides, like a boxer gaining momentum to throw a punch. I rested my hand on the table to steady myself.

Patrick snarled.

"You never do what you are told to do. You never listen. That's your damn problem. Bitch."

In my mind I began to run. I wasn't running away from something as much as I was just trying to get to a place where nothing could touch me. I ran until I couldn't feel anything anymore.

Images of the train and conversations with Jim shot in and out of my mind, but I forced myself to concentrate on reality. In that fire house, in that room, all my exits were blocked. In that room, where there was seemingly less air by the second, I was trapped. I momentarily thought that if Patrick moved his arm toward me one more time, I was just going to run and hope that I was faster than they were. I flinched as his voice reached a new level of anger. I felt like I was losing my spark, as if Patrick's voice was a needle draining the life out of me. I began to breathe deeper, faster. All the other firefighters were outside in the back parking lot cutting junk cars apart and I was sure that no one would hear me scream. I was also sure that Patrick and Ray had planned it that way.

I believe that there is a unique strength in *all* people, fierce and hidden. Some rarely need to use it, some get it all in a rush at the needed moment. Some people have a practiced power that they have learned to harness over time. Mine came to me in a way that I did not foresee. Keeping my voice even but loud, I spoke over Patrick.

"Please. I am really sorry. I didn't mean to offend you in anyway. I didn't mean to disrespect you." My palms faced Patrick's chest as if I was preparing to push him away. "That isn't what happened, though. You were standing right next to me, that didn't happen!"

I was talking to Patrick, but looking at Ray. He was glancing at the floor, my shoe, the clock behind my head. I dared him to look at me, to look into my eyes and witness what he was allowing to happen. I could see that I had surprised Patrick, his eyes widened as if he did not expect me to talk back to him. That gave me a strange sense of satisfaction, and my body was flooded with a level of disgust I hadn't ever felt before.

Patrick saw that he was in complete control. He saw that Ray was going to let him go as far as he wanted to. Patrick spat the words at me. "Well, if it is so hard for you here, then maybe you should just avoid the problem altogether. You are not capable of being a firefighter, of being here with us. How else can we tell you? You do not belong. You know what? You shouldn't be allowed to ride on any call until you prove yourself."

As I opened my mouth to yell, "You call yourselves firefighters, but this is a joke to you! You don't train, you don't even try to do well at this job," I was abruptly aware of my heart beating solidly in my chest. The thud-thud resonated in my ears. I knew it was my adrenaline kicking in, preparing me to battle or run. I also took it as a sign that I was still alive, still a contender in this fight. It dawned on me then that this would never stop until I quit. These people were never going to stop trying to intimidate me and bury me in rules until I was gone. On the heels of that thought came, *No. No way. I am not quitting this.*

Ray finally chimed in, making an unrelated comment to Patrick and they started to have a conversation about something, as if they had just bumped into each other on the street. I was standing there silent and stunned, gazing back and forth between two men whom I had once trusted my safety to. Ray turned to me.

"You know, Ali, you should really work on trusting more people in the fire company. They want what's best for you." That comment was so absurd I almost laughed out loud. They conveniently made all the problems my fault. Ray and Patrick made faces like they were mentally high-fiving each other and then began to make their way to the door. I couldn't move. I was so angry I literally could not move. Over his shoulder, Ray called out, "You know, Pat has always been the one to stand up for you."

I was not allowed to show my fury. In the clearest way I knew how, I tried to get them to hear me. I stepped in front of them to stop them from walking away from me.

"Please. Please stop this. I am not the person you are making me out to be. I am just trying to... You had the right to earn a place here, why don't I?"

I walked out of the room after them, tripping over my foolish words. But they tumbled out into a world that could not contain us all. This was the first night that I realized Ray was not on my side. He never had been. He just couldn't hide it anymore. Ray had to choose a side and he chose to oppose me.

I walked out to where Will and Evan were watching the training. Will noticed my face and without any words being spoken, he knew he needed to help me get balanced again. He motioned to the Jaws of Life being used in the vehicle training and did his best to get me refocused.

"See how he is holding the Jaws?"

I looked and nodded.

"Make sure to never put your body in between them and the car when you are cutting, 'cause if the Jaws start to grab the metal in the wrong way, you could be in trouble."

I nodded again, mentally storing that piece of information.

Despite Will's attempt to get me focused on the training, I knew that I would not be able to display my happy façade to everyone else, so I left the station. Some days I just didn't feel like fighting.

I mumbled a few words to my family and shut myself away. Sitting on the floor in the dark with my back against my bed, I waited patiently for the release of the tears, but they never came. I grew surprised, knowing that it was not like me. I was stinging inside and then just went numb, like my body was all out of feelings to feel. Suddenly I yanked a pillow from my bed and clutched it to my face. I was trying to contain what I could no longer hold, but I felt the scream before I heard it. It was a horror-movie type of scream that came from incoherent anger. I screamed so loud for so long that my throat felt like it was being sliced open by a million butcher's knives. I only stopped to gather enough breath to begin to scream again. The pillow became soaked with tears, sweat, and spit. My breath rattled in and out like it physically hurt me to breathe.

Jim appeared in my mind. "Ali."

Still sitting across from him on the train, my eyes were cloudy as I looked up at him.

"There is no limit to what you can dream, or understand, or have faith in. There is no limit to how much you can handle. There is no limit to how much you can love something. There is no limit. You can deal with this."

Reassured, I began to breathe more steadily. Jim's words helped to get my head back above the surface, but now I was like a level whose bubble sat just off center.

* * *

I was in high school throughout all of this. Mentally I was busy fighting with myself. I was basically just faking my way through life. I wasn't really living, because I was living so directly for only one thing. My last two years of high school were difficult. I knew I was losing friends, but I couldn't make myself care about what they talked about. A friend called to invite me to the movies, but I had just gotten back from a call and was too frustrated to be around people. I said no to the movie and eventually, people stopped asking.

A few days later I sat at my kitchen table staring at a math problem, doing my best to stay present in the world. The fire pager hung heavy at my side. When I heard calls come across, even the ones that I used to dream of, I didn't move except to cover my face with my hands. My mom wrapped her arms around me, and kissed my head. Tears didn't even come. They could bring no relief. But there it was, that feeling of emptiness, of invisibility and invalidation.

I believe in the integrity of firefighters for the sole reason that my heart always knew it was the truth. And maybe it is just a feeling that you are chasing. Yes, it might seem absurd to plan your entire life around a feeling, but you don't have to be able to explain it. You just have to be able to make something of it. I trusted that convincing little voice I heard when I was firefighting. We all live our lives based on beliefs. We believe in things we can't see, things whose existence we cannot prove. We believe that nothing devastating will happen to us, we believe that we are never given more than we can handle, we believe that the sun will always rise in the morning. The darkness always gets erased by the light.

* * *

I began to take a class called The Essentials of Firefighting. It was a seven-month-long firefighting class that taught skills from the most basic to the final test, which involved putting out a real fire. Instead of focusing on my senior year of high school, I threw myself into the Essentials class. Firefighting was what mattered to me.

Firefighting is a privilege. We have the opportunity to positively affect lives. It is not something to be taken lightly. I now realized that most of the people in my fire company wasted this opportunity. It took me time to realize that the fire house operated in a way that was entirely different from the rest of my universe. It was a world where fine didn't mean fine and nothing was black and white, but various shades of red. I was not allowed to show emotion because that would only give them what they wanted. It would prove to them that women are too emotional, that we cannot be strong. Early on I learned how to close my heart like a fist, so I didn't feel so much. After enough time of living this way, your body turns into a marble statue, cold and hard. With the next damaging touch you splinter, unable to shatter completely. From the outside you look whole, but inside you are nothing but a million fractured pieces that are barely holding themselves together.

I was sitting in English class one morning when I heard the echo of a fire truck siren a few blocks away. I knew there was a call and wanted to spring out of my seat and go to join the other firefighters in the world where things actually mattered. But as the sound of the siren faded away, I felt a strange tear in my heart and was filled with a new kind of bottomless sorrow. I felt myself slipping farther away. I was becoming a martyr, dying spiritually rather than giving up on my dream. I was just a ghost of myself, filled with shadows of the person I used to be.

* * *

A daughter of one of the firefighters and her friends sat in my study hall. I pushed the iPod headphones far into my ears, but each time the song changed and silence filled my head, I heard them talking. The words "slut," "whore," and "skank" filtered into my mind as they talked about me. Other kids were looking in my direction, I felt their questioning stares. I wasn't free anywhere.

* * *

Tones dropped for a chimney fire. I started off the call in a bad mood because I was angry about always getting in trouble. However, with each call that came, I had faith that it would be the call to turn things around. I got up from the chair I was sitting in, got keys and shoes, and went to the fire house. There were a few people getting ready when I walked in the door and we slowly got in the engine without speaking to each other.

There wasn't much to do when we arrived on scene. The fire had been contained to the fireplace.

I was standing around watching firefighters place a ladder on the side of the house when someone asked a firefighter with a sense of humor what time it was.

He said, "Oh, I dunno, like 10:30."

I stopped. "Wait, what?" I really hoped I heard him wrong.

He checked again. "It's like 10:30."

I stared at him until he got it. Finally, he smiled, shook my hand and said, "Well, see ya in thirty days."

Everyone knew that I was not allowed to run fire calls after 10 p.m. Everyone had remembered this, except for me. I did not even look at the time when the tones went, I was just so used to leaving whatever I was doing and going to the station. I instantly hated myself for breaking a rule that I actually knew about. Most of the time I was just "breaking rules" that people made up on the spot. But I knew about this one.

I walked into a shadow where the bright lights and intrusive stares could no longer reach me. I closed my eyes and pressed my cheek against the gold-leafed letters spelling F-I-R-E on the side of the truck. I waited for the feeling to come, for that ocean of anguish in my stomach to rise up and slowly take me over, stronger with each breaking wave. I saw him then, another firefighter standing up the street from me. He had been watching. He had his feet spread wide apart and his arms were crossed, guarding his massive chest. His head was cocked slightly to the side like he was trying to find the answer to something.

My expression changed to embarrassment. I hated that he caught me showing such obvious signs of weakness. I knew what I had done, but my eyes were pleading with him to show me some kind of mercy.

As the light bulb clicked on in his head, he marched down past me to find Chief Ray. He grabbed his arm. They walked down the block and had a discussion in nothing but whispers. The street was dark, except for the invasive lights from the fire trucks. As they flashed, the light lit up the men's faces and I tried to make out what they were saying. Every other word seemed to be my name.

When we got back to the station, no one talked except to say what was absolutely necessary.

"You took my flashlight."

"Where did you put my I.D. tag?"

Other than that, there was just silence. I immediately went to the rule book, where the pages on junior firefighters were so worn I could pick them out and flip right to them. According to the rules, since it was a Friday night and I didn't have school the next day, apparently I could respond to calls up until midnight. So, small crisis averted. A kind firefighter came up to me and smiled, trying to patch the holes in my crumbling composure. I wanted to smile back, but instead, I just walked to my locker, slammed my helmet into it and watched it ricochet off the sides. I ripped my gear off and didn't put it back together before kicking it into the locker. My anger threatened to bubble over as I slammed open the station door and walked outside. I wanted to sleep until the day when they wouldn't remember me.

The lines had been drawn. Friendships between the firefighters that had existed for more than twenty years were collapsing because one person was for me and one was against me. But certain people like Jared and Ricky, who used to make their hatred for each other public, had bonded over their disgust of me. I wanted everyone to know that I was staying. I never allowed myself to entertain the thought of leaving this way. But every night when I walked into that fire house, they looked at me like I was naked. It didn't matter how many sweatshirts I wore or how many sizes too big the clothes were, the feeling of overexposure remained.

I spent a lot of time dozing in the in-between pond, with sleep on one shore and reality on the other. It was a place where the edges of life didn't feel so sharp but I was still alert enough to be in control of my own thoughts. I lay in bed, and while I waited for sleep I softly sang a song into the darkness. I was so grateful that someone else had found a way to put into words what I was feeling. My voice carried out into the darkness, barely above a whisper: *"I've started feeling like I don't want to fight. Just give in to the given, and put out the light."*

Chapter 5

To Pieces

I am convinced that anyone can survive anything, as long as they believe there will be a point to their suffering, as long as one day there will be a reason for it all.

* * *

One evening in early spring, my fire company was paged to assist the ambulance with an overdose in the woods. Those calls are pretty rare, so I was excited at the chance to do something new. After we all clambered into the rescue, we flew down the road with the ambulance right behind us. I loaded extra rubber gloves into my pockets and made sure I had my CPR pocket mask in my gear. We arrived at a clearing in the woods at the entrance to a popular hiking trail. Evan was on the radio with Dispatch trying to determine where exactly on the mountain our patient was. He was in charge of the call, also known as the Incident Commander or the "I.C." We didn't know what the patient had overdosed on or whether or not she was still alive. Some hikers had found her and at the time of their 9-1-1 call, she was still alive.

I helped Will unload the Stokes basket from the back of the rescue as the evening sun beat down on us. (A Stokes basket is a backboard in a metal frame. The metal curls out around the sides to provide handles for the firefighters. It is used for rescues where the terrain is less than ideal.) We were all in head-to-toe firefighting gear, since upon arrival we didn't know we would need to hike to reach our patient.

Hiking up a mountain with a Stokes basket is tiring enough without having the extra pounds of gear weighing on us. We left our coats in a pile on the ground near Evan, and began the hike up the mountain.

Our portable radios crackled. I heard Evan asking for more manpower to the scene. Sweat began to collect around the waistband of my sweatpants. We hiked for minutes in silence, looking at the ground for stubborn rocks waiting to trip us. People began to switch positions so some could take a break from carrying the basket. I stayed at the front and never let go. My legs burnt with exhaustion as we trekked higher and higher between the trees. I no longer trusted the men in my fire house. I didn't trust them to do everything they could to save this woman's life. The dying sunlight shone through the breaks in the trees and silhouetted us against the side of the mountain.

Evan had told us to walk until we located the patient, but I began to worry that we wouldn't ever find her. No one knew how much time she had left. Finally we came upon a girl lying in a pink and grey sleeping bag in the middle of the trail. I hesitated for a millisecond longer than the others. The sight of her face made me realize the gravity of the situation. Will bumped into my arm as he rushed past me. Following him, I knelt in the dirt and dry leaves next to her body. I almost cried knowing what she had done, knowing how close she was to not existing, knowing that unlike the others, she did not want to be saved.

The hikers that found the woman looked relieved as we arrived. After they called 9-1-1, they picked the woman up and carried her down the mountain as far as they could.

My eyes went to her chest, searching for any signs of breath entering or exiting her lungs. It was there, faintly. We lifted the dying woman into the basket and Will and I tied her in securely with rescue rope. Turning back the way we came, we began to walk. It took a while to get used to carrying the weight of a person; it had been hard enough to make it up the mountain with just the weight of the basket alone. We worked to get into a rhythm with each other.

The muscles in my lower back screamed in resistance as my foot slipped off a rock and my body twisted. We all struggled to keep the Stokes basket upright. It was getting harder to grasp the metal handles as my sweaty hands made the inside of my gloves slippery. The woman in the basket was oblivious to this as we tried to protect her unconscious body from the prickly branches that reached out to scratch our arms and faces. Darkness was beginning to obscure the path down the mountain, so we all pulled out our flashlights and tried to light the way. Firefighters not carrying the basket walked ahead and held back low-hanging tree branches and warned the rest about rocks. Occasionally one of us would stumble and fall to our knees, having caught the toe of our boot on a rock protruding from the ground. The group would stop momentarily and after that person said a few curse words, he would get to his feet and we would continue. A tree branch cut my face and as more sweat formed, the cut stung.

The trail seemed endless on the way back down and my body was nearing its limit of physical strain. I could feel that my face was flushed with physical exertion. I wondered aloud why we hadn't brought any water bottles. When the pain in my back or arms would get to be almost too much, I would look down at the woman's ashen face and tell myself that it did not matter how sore I was the next day, it didn't matter if I couldn't walk for a week, I needed to keep putting one foot in front of the other. I kept peering ahead, hoping to see the flashing light of the emergency vehicles I knew were waiting for us at the base of the mountain. There was a distant rumbling sound and I saw one of the firefighters riding toward us on an ATV. I had no idea where he had gotten it, but it did not matter as we placed the Stokes basket across the back. Exhausted, we held the woman steady as the firefighter pressed the gas. We saw the lights of the emergency vehicles waiting at the bottom of the mountain. We sped up, like runners in sight of their finish line. The woman was delivered to the waiting medics who took over her care.

I helped to get the woman out alive. I told myself that was the only thing I had control over. How sad this woman must have been to walk up into the woods, take a couple dozen pills, curl up into a sleeping bag and wait to die.

* * *

It was time for the monthly company meeting at the fire house. Every week there were new rules to further restrict me. New committees were formed under seemingly appropriate titles but they really just groups of firefighters sitting around in the fire house, discussing my supposed faults. It had gotten to the point where any firefighter could make up anything about how I performed on a call and it would not be challenged, no matter how absurd the accusation. "Failure to follow directions." "Demeaning the image of the fire company." I couldn't help but roll my eyes. I kept lists of all the rule proposals to date to try to keep up with them and of everything I was being blamed for.

In that particular meeting, Jared sat with his big tattooed arms crossed, hiding behind his tinted sunglasses. Someone asked him an innocent question, trying to get him to join in on the discussion and break the tension in the room. He responded with, "I would answer you, but I don't want someone to think it was harassment." Every head in the room snapped toward me, like soldiers moving to attention.

And then a flower of hate bloomed inside of me. It began inside my rib cage and grew up my spine, choking my bitter heart. Blossoming in my face, it splashed red across my cheeks. I hated Jared with every ounce of strength that my body possessed. My finger began to tap out a broken beat along the inseam of my jeans. My outlet was hidden to the multiple sets of eyes fastened upon me. I bit down on my lip until the metallic taste of blood startled me enough to make me stop. I hated Jared for pursuing me like he did. I hated him for everything. I hated him for making me lose my sense of security in the world. I couldn't seem to get it back. I couldn't get any of it back. I could not get the feeling of hatred to go away. I looked without seeing, smiled without feeling, lived without faith.

I lifted weights until I could no longer raise my arms, until I thought I could literally feel the muscle ripping away from the bone. I filled garbage bags full of ice and draped them over my sore and screaming body. I always gave up exhausted, seeing no point in killing myself for a profession that didn't want me anyway. From recent search training, I had a string of bruises down my shins. They started dark brown and faded to light green, wounds of the secret life I led.

I graduated from high school about this time. I forced myself to partake in some of the standard end-of-high-school activities: an excursion to a nearby amusement park, and skipping school on senior skip day. Laughter and happiness surrounded me as classmates enjoyed our last days of high school. I stood there as we waited to proceed into the auditorium to receive our diplomas. I stood there with so much hurt inside of me and I tried my best to be normal. Nothing could fill the void that was present. Nothing could mend my broken heart.

I received my black helmet too. This color of helmet signified to all firefighters that I had passed certain firefighting tests and that I was eighteen and could perform all functions on a fire ground. I had finally received the symbol of achievement I had been waiting for, but all I cared about was the world I was being kicked out of. Unfortunately, there is no easy remedy for a broken heart, no matter the reason for the breaking.

* * *

One of the most difficult aspects of the whole situation was that the firefighters never said things to my face. When I would walk into the fire house, people just moved out of my way like if they got too close they would catch whatever disease I had that made me so repulsive. It was all portrayed in the looks they gave me, in their answers to questions I'd asked or in rumors that I had heard about myself. I was really practiced at dealing with that type of hidden hatred, the kind that never showed its face to me directly. I really did feel brave. My anger was there as usual, annoying me like the grumble of an upset stomach. I was also determined to continue on living.

I wanted to go down to the local arts festival and sit in the tent provided for the fire company to do overnight security and study for my final in Essentials class, which was my structure burn. So I did.

I walked up to the tent, noticing that Patrick and Ricky were the only ones on duty. I spread my books out on the table, putting up all kinds of invisible walls around myself. This was my attempt at protection. Patrick and Ricky started talking to each other in that loud way that people do when they want other people to overhear. One of them said that there were certain people that should have been kicked out of the fire company a long time ago. My eyes were focused on a page about flame rollover when I heard them stand up behind me. Patrick's voice, like a dull blade, cut into me.

"People in this fire company get away with things they shouldn't. People aren't punished."

I stayed in the chair with my back to them, silently waiting.

"You should know the truth about what people think of you."

Placing the book down on the table, I spun around to face them. Arrogantly, Ricky looked me up and down.

"Let me spell it out for you. You are a failure. You fail. You can't do this job and you never could. We just let you stay here because you are good entertainment. Why the hell do you even try anymore? You're a whore, that's obvious. Just leave."

Patrick sneered, hatred gleamed in his eyes. "You shouldn't be here, Allllli."

The anger I had been suppressing rose to the surface.

"Enough! Enough. I can't...I am not what you say I am! I don't do those things! What is wrong with you that you keep making up these lies?"

My anger grew serious as my voice became flat. I spoke with as much hate as I could muster, trying to match them.

"I didn't sleep with anyone and you know it."

I turned back to the table and began shoving all my books back into my backpack. I had to get away.

Before I could take a step in the direction of my car, Will and his wife came hustling through the trees. I started to walk, to get away. Will gave me a questioning look and reached out to stop me, but I just shook my head. I was too close to losing control. All the emotion I had forced myself to bury deep inside was threatening to come out in a flood of tears. I rushed to my car, trying to look like I wasn't rushing because I was fine, and things like this happened to me all the time. I pulled out of the parking lot and turned right, the shortest way home.

I pulled into the driveway and parked the car slightly sideways. I stumbled out, dragging my backpack behind me. The emotion I struggled with daily was fighting to escape. I tripped up the steps, raised my arm and threw my backpack against the kitchen wall as hard as I could. The books slammed into the wall and tumbled out onto the floor. When I was in the bathroom, where I could lock the door, I held my hands to my face, trying to hide the tears my body could no longer hold. They seeped through the cracks between my fingers and trickled down my knuckles. Like a small hole in a big dam, all my emotion came pouring out and I cried until there was nothing left in me. Blinking, I felt the tears chase each other down my cheeks. They followed the flare of my nose and curled around my mouth. I felt them soundlessly drop, hitting the bare skin peeking out from the top of my shirt, the skin that I tried so carefully to hide. I screamed out angrily, my fists pounded into my thighs. I was melting into a puddle of nothing. I knew I would have to talk to someone soon, so I began to take big deep breaths. I soaked my face with water, trying to camouflage the tears. My phone beeped; text message from Will. He had called an emergency meeting of the chiefs at the fire station. He wanted me to come and tell my side of the story. Knowing that I would break down completely in front of them, I said no. They would later take this action as an admission of guilt.

Shortly after receiving the text message, I heard two cars pull up outside my house. It was Will, his wife Sara, and Evan. They marched up my driveway, a line of soldiers. I opened the door for them, but could not look up from the ground. The entire time they talked, I kept my eyes on my hands. I knew that if I looked into their eyes and saw their pity for me, those tears would leak out again.

Will tried to re-spark my motivation. "So you have your burn tomorrow? That's exciting!"

"It *was* exciting. I don't care anymore."

"No, Ali." Sara's blonde hair bounced gently as she shook her head. She spoke strong and clear. "Don't let them take this from you."

Will said that Ray mentioned the fire company wanted to suspend Patrick, Ricky and me for the altercation because then no one had to pick a side.

After they left, I didn't have to wait long for Jim to appear. The familiar train seat curved to fit my back as I leaned heavily into it.

"It's me against them, Jim. They will win, every time."

Jim thought for a moment, trying to decide exactly how to respond.

"There are so many struggles in this world. I know you feel many of them in yourself. But sometimes you can't look at the world and its problems because it seems too much to fix. You have to look at your world and change the things you can. Then you can take it higher."

I spoke desperately but from the heart. "I want to change the world. But I don't know how. I get scared about going through life and having no impact. Of being known as nothing but a monster."

Jim took the pressure off. "You have to remind yourself that this is not your battle. This is not your war. It is not your job to change anything. All you have to do is express qualities like humility, gratitude, generosity, and grace. We need to be the kind of people we want to see more of."

The next day came too soon. It was time for my structure burn. It was the last day of my seven-month-long Essentials firefighting class. We loaded up the burn building with excelsior hay, which is used to accelerate the fire's growth

I had the first burn evolution of the day. I found my burn partner and the instructor who would accompany us inside to fight the fire. There was a team of firefighters stationed outside the main door, ready to come in and get us if things got out of control. I was nervous. I felt the familiar pressure, the weight in my heart. The fire was lit on the inside, the smoke began to push from the cracks around the windows. I picked a hose; my partner loaded it onto his shoulder. The burn instructor briefed us at the door. I looked up and saw heavy smoke pushing through the ventilation holes in the top floor. I saw the dark stairwell just inside the door. We connected the regulator to our face pieces, took a breath and stepped inside to the point of no return.

My partner went up the stairs with the instructor. I stayed back and ran the length of the hose, making sure there were no kinks in it. I flaked it out in big loops against the wall, so I just had to push one loop forward and the team in the fire room would have more hose. My partner yelled for water and as the engine driver outside obliged, the hose became rock solid. I checked it quickly, the flow was uninterrupted. As I walked toward the fire, I opened all the windows I passed. Smoke rushed out above my head. As a team, we advanced toward the fire. The hose was manageable in my hands. I used the weight of my body to pull it around. The burn instructor had us sit and watch the fire grow. The flames began to roll across the ceiling, over our heads. The amount of heat was growing exponentially. The burn instructor told us to put out the fire, then my partner and I switched positions. I was now in charge of the nozzle. It was my job to put out the remaining fire.

There was a fire burning in the attic. Our crew crawled up the steps, yanking the hose behind us, keeping to one side of the staircase. As I reached the top of the stairs, I felt the heat coming at me from the right. With the hose held tightly to my body, I pushed off the stair railing with my foot and rolled around onto my left side. I opened the nozzle and hit the fire without standing up, therefore avoiding the majority of the heat and saving my remaining energy.

After the fire was out, I broke down the couplings in the hose and loaded it onto my shoulder to make it easier to carry. Water trickled down the hallway past my feet. While walking down the steps, the quarter service alarm sounded on my air pack, which meant that my air cylinder was low on air. I felt the vibration and could just make out the sound of the bell that accompanied it. I disconnected my air regulator and kept it from swinging with my right hand. With my left hand I reached behind me to shut off the dwindling air supply. I immediately dressed out of my gear. After all, it was July.

While I was walking over to get my air pack serviced, my burn instructor caught up with me. He pulled me aside. I began to get worried. I replayed the fire in my mind to figure out what I did wrong.

The instructor spoke. "Well, I don't often tell young people this, you know, especially when they are just starting out. But I would go into a fire with you any day. I was very impressed. You just didn't quit in there. I was very proud of you."

My heart soared.

* * *

About this time, I needed to start studying to take my Firefighter 1 test. Being certified as a Firefighter 1 is the first major certification all firefighters strive for. Our basic skills are tested, like setting ladders against a building, searching through a maze for an imaginary victim, and cutting a hole in a roof to stop the fire from spreading. Mentally, I was nowhere near ready for the test, but I had been signed up to take it through my Essentials class. More prominent in my mind was the disciplinary committee meeting to prepare for after the incident with Patrick and Ricky.

My parents had decided that they were going to attend the meeting too, and before it even started, people had problems with that. My dad calmly told the committee that they were simply there to make sure that I was treated fairly. The firefighters started reading the complaints that had been lodged against me. Ricky and Patrick said that they were just trying to have an innocent conversation with me, and that I made the conversation turn ugly. They said that I embarrassed and belittled not only them, but the entire fire company. As the complaints were read, the firefighters in the meeting nodded along in agreement. I saw the amusement on their faces. They were doing this simply as an absurd formality in front of my parents. Then they gave me an opportunity to read my statement. When I did my voice was shaky. The meeting ended with me deciding that I simply had nothing more to say. My Firefighter 1 test was scheduled for the upcoming weekend and I had to focus on that. I felt I simply had to pass to prove once and for all that I was competent.

Just a week later, it was time, and the day began early. The students milled around the testing ground, eager and ready to start. My burn instructor was there and pulled me aside by the arm. He looked at me, hard and commiserating. "Ali, you *have* to calm down."

I was fluttering around him, unable to stand still. In my head I cried out, *You don't understand. I have to pass. I need to pass. If I don't pass, I will never be able to get out of this town.* I wanted to tell him, *You have no idea what this is doing to me. Please, just help me pass.* Instead, I just meekly nodded. The contents of my small breakfast were threatening to come back up.

The day began. When I was told who I was partnered with, my spirits dropped. Through each test station, I did all of the work. I knew my partner was not capable of performing well enough to pass out of each station, and if one failed, we both did. So we went along, with me always taking the harder of the two jobs. Then the hose line advancement station came. As a team, we had to climb a ladder to the second floor with a load of hose over our shoulders. One had to crawl with the hose down a hallway and extinguish an imaginary fire. All the other partner had to do was climb the ladder after the first firefighter entered the window and make sure that the hose line did not kink up. I balanced the load on my right shoulder and looked up to the second floor. It seemed like such a long way to the top. Before I left the ground, I spelled it out for my partner.

"Wait until I'm in the window, then start to climb. Before you climb through the window, sound the floor. The evaluator will be looking for that. I am going to drop the hose load inside the window, make sure you flake it out all the way. Then crawl down the hall after me."

He nodded to me and I began to climb the ladder. I did what I was supposed to do. When my partner showed up behind me, I asked if the hose was flaked out and he said yes. I called for water. No water came. Why? The hose was still in the pile I had left at the bottom of the window. Both of us failed that station. It was the same story the whole day. And it ended with me failing two stations because of my partner, and one station due to my own error and inexperience.

It was the roof simulator that got me. It was a giant piece of wood about 6 feet off the ground and slanted from the top to the bottom. The station required the firefighter to climb the simulated roof on a ladder and cut a four-sided hole with an inspection cut; three cuts with a chainsaw, two with an axe. I made it through the evolution, but took too long to do it. As the evaluator pulled me aside and told me that I could come back the next day to try again, I felt myself falling deeper. The evaluator told me that he was really impressed with what I was doing, being a girl among all the guys. That hadn't been a source of reassurance to me in a very long time. I nodded without really hearing what he said, agreeing to come back.

The next day came much too soon and I found myself standing in front of the roof simulator again. With the crowd of evaluators standing behind me, I pulled hard on the chainsaw. It started with one pull. I placed the ladder on the roof simulator, along with the hook and axe. I sounded the roof and climbed back down. I grabbed the saw and climbed with it to the roof. It started easily, and I made the three required cuts. Only two more cuts with the axe and I was free. I placed the saw off to the side and grabbed the axe. I swung it up, over my shoulder. I stepped back and put all my weight on my left foot. My right foot slipped off the ladder rung and I felt myself start to fall. I dropped the axe and tried to grab the ladder rung in front of me. A helpless cry escaped me as I realized I was going to fall. I watched the ground come to meet my face, knowing that whatever happened next was going to hurt. It didn't happen slowly like in the movies, if anything, time seemed to fast forward. I closed my eyes just before I hit, already giving in to the pain before it came.

With a foggy mind, I felt someone hold my neck still. Someone else said, "look at her arm." That caused me to vaguely focus on my right arm which I could feel was bent unnaturally under my body. Later the instructors told me that my shoulder had dislocated when I landed, and when they rolled me onto my back it went back into place.

I don't remember getting up to walk, but I ended up inside one of the old burn rooms. One of the instructors came in, cracking open an ice pack in his hands. Placing it on my shoulder and cheek, he stood back to look at me. His face was drawn tight. I wanted to tell him that I didn't fall off on purpose, and to please not be mad, but my mouth was dry and my thoughts were blurred. Instructors and evaluators were coming into the room from all over the site. I sat there, leaning heavily on the wooden chair as if I were on display. I licked my lips and they tasted bitter. I panicked for a split second, thinking that something in my mouth was bleeding but then I realized that the ice pack had split open and I was tasting the saltiness of the chemicals inside. I dropped it to the ground. Will walked in, took one look at me and said that I was done, no more fire. I stared out the window at the piece of wood that was left uncut. Someone placed their hand on my back and helped me stand. I did not want to, but I had to hold onto his arm to steady myself as I stood. Checking for any obvious injuries to my ribs, one of the instructors pulled up my dark blue shirt to reveal skin as white as a flag of surrender.

"Alright Ali, lift your arm."

I raised my right arm a few inches, grimaced and stopped.

"Can you make a fist?"

Skin stretched tight across my knuckles as I did what he asked.

Checking me for signs of a concussion, he asked, "What day is it?"

"My Firefighter 1 day," I said quietly and closed my eyes. I did not cry. I did not feel anything but the growing pain that was spreading from my right ear to my right hip.

Will drove me home, calling my parents on the way. I shifted in the seat next to him as I tried to find a position that was comfortable. Angrily, I tugged at the seat belt that hugged my shoulder too tightly.

Will held the phone away from his mouth to talk to me. "Take it easy."

My dad met us in the driveway and I was whisked away to the hospital. Because I was injured on fire academy property, it was mandatory that I was checked by a doctor. With my dad supporting most of my weight, we walked slowly through the automatic doors of the emergency room.

In the ER, I felt the nurse's hands on the sides of my head to hold it still. The rigid collar was placed around my neck and I felt intense pressure in my head. The white emergency room was beginning to spin. The sickening smell of the hospital was beginning to make my stomach turn. I felt the prickly fabric of the hospital pillow scratch my neck. As my dad and I waited for the doctor's arrival, I heard his breath catch in his throat. Unable to turn my head, I reached my hand down to him and he held it securely between his. We stayed like that for a while.

"Oh honey," came his voice, as soft as a prayer. "I'm so sorry."

I left the hospital with my arm in a sling. Each time I looked down and saw it, I knew I was totally and completely broken down, inside and out. I lay in bed that night, my ribs hurting each time I breathed. My shoulder throbbed.

As soon as I let my mind go, I found myself on the train. In my mind, darkness was falling abruptly the way a curtain comes down at the end of the second act.

Jim looked at me intently, waiting for me to talk first. His long fingers splayed on his cheek as his elbow sat on the arm rest.

"Pretty great, huh?" I asked sarcastically, nodding down to my arm. The sling wasn't there but my arm sat rigidly in my lap like a bird protecting an injured wing.

Jim didn't seem to notice. "How are you?"

I waited a few moments before avoiding his question. I stared down at my arm. The angry words I planned to say went out of my mind. "What's wrong with me?" I asked quietly. "Why do I still love this after all they've done?"

Jim chuckled in disagreement. "There is nothing wrong with you. Look, you still want to be a firefighter, right?"

"Of course, that's never changed. But I feel so stuck, so suspended in the past and I can't get beyond it. I can't believe that I still want this and it's killing me to stay. I'm lost. I'm so lost." My eyes welled with emotion.

Jim spoke lovingly. "Ali, it is so easy to love the idea of something, or to love it from a distance. It is easy to sit in the comfort of your home or your town and dream and dream and wish for the future. But you have to have the courage and bravery to go up to your dreams and take them. No one will hand you your dream the way you want it. So do it yourself. Imagine if you succeeded at everything you attempted.

Imagine if you got everything you wanted. Not only would life be boring, we would all be incredibly spoiled. It is important to have something to fight for, some greater purpose beyond yourself."

Satisfied that he had gotten his point across, Jim turned back to the book he held in his hands. His pen was poised above the page briefly, but then he began to scribble something down.

I thought for a while.

"Jim?"

"Hmm?" He did not look up from the page.

"I still don't know if I can do this."

"All you have to do is ask yourself two questions. What do you believe in? And how hard are you willing to fight for it?"

* * *

The next day, I found out that Ray had resigned as fire chief of the company. Earlier that week, my parents had asked him to give them written proof of the steps he said he had been taking to ensure that I was not being singled out at the fire house. The buildup of the past year was weighing too heavily on him and he chose to walk away. Sam was going to take his place as chief until elections could be held that upcoming December.

* * *

I sat on Will's front porch in a one-person hammock that hung from the roof supports. My bare feet dangled beneath me in the evening summer breeze. I felt a small release of the pressure that I carried around daily. Sara walked out from the kitchen, three root beers in hand. Will and I talked about everything that was happening, about the disappointment we felt toward these people and the uncertainty about our futures in that fire house. Will had grown up with these men. They went to high school together and they have lived in the same town all their lives. I never really knew these men as honorable people. But Will did. Their actions were even more upsetting to him. I figured this division within the fire company was just what happened when one lived his or her life in a constant state of war.

The only defense against hate is love.

Chapter 6

The Dark Night

"My forehead is still bleeding from the thorns I used to wear.
And I'm left alone and beaten for this cross I choose to bear."
HANSON, *When You're Gone*

* * *

Will and I had plans to visit a different fire department on the outskirts of a nearby city. Will was checking it out to see if he wanted to become a firefighter there to run calls on the weekends and I was tagging along to hang out with the firefighters and get to know another fire station. We were going to stay for three days. Most fire stations have a program called "riding along" where firefighters from other companies ride calls without participating to get a feel for a different station. I felt like this trip could make or break me, but I was determined to continue fighting. I made the three-hour drive with Will, hoping more than anything that this would be a fire house where I fit in.

Early in the morning I had just returned to the station after a bloody car accident on the highway. A man had been driving a box truck containing furniture, lost control, and rolled it over onto its side. He managed to climb out of the driver's side door; there were bloody handprints to prove it. In the wreckage, he had severed the carotid artery in his neck. By the time firefighters arrived, passersby had already stopped and had their hands clamped over his neck. When the medics attempted to move him from the pavement to the stretcher and pressure was released from his neck, the man had a seizure. Small puddles of blood lay in the road like water after a sudden rain storm. I stood there watching the bizarre and graphic scene, unable to help since I was just an observer. I clutched a box of rubber gloves in my hands.

I was sitting in the kitchen when some firefighters came back to the station after a long night of partying. I moved into the lounge and tried to hide myself in the darkness. I figured I would just wait for them to go upstairs and then I would follow them to the bunk room and go to sleep. I sat in the dark, waiting. I heard them enter the room, laughing and tripping over each other. I didn't think they noticed me on the couch, but they stopped to laugh at a perverse joke. They were so close I was trying to quiet my breathing, but I was discovered. One sat down on my right, laughing hysterically and yanking at my hair. The other two came at me from the left. I leaned back to get away and found myself in the lap of the person on my right. Arms and legs were everywhere as I struggled, unable to get out from under them. I felt paralyzing pressure on my neck as fingers dug into my throat. I opened my mouth to scream but no sound escaped. Drunken laughter roared in my ear drums. Choking, sickening alcohol-flavored breath smothered me. I had time for just one thought. *I can't breathe.* I didn't just mean in the literal sense. This world was suffocating me.

A moment later, a rough touch on the skin of my stomach was like an electric charge that shocked me with enough energy to get out from under them. As I ran through the dark fire station, their laughter and boozy breath echoed after me. I tore down the hallway, through the double doors leading to the truck bay, and past a group of people sitting on the couches behind the quiet trucks. The drunken firefighters called after me to come back. I burst loudly into the bunk room trying to get to Will, to safety, to a place where I could shut the door. Bunk beds lined the walls and I made my way through the maze of them. I sat down heavily on an unoccupied bed and gripped the bedspread. I closed my eyes and couldn't help but think of their hands all over my body. From across the room, Will sat up and saw my face through the dark.

"Hey. You okay?"

Breathe. "Yeah," I said, in the way that meant no. *Breathe.*

"Bad call?"

"Yeah. Bad call." Telling a lie was easier than reliving the past. I was so used to being blamed for everything. I believed somehow this would be seen as my fault too.

"Want to talk about it?"

"No."

"Try to get some sleep."

"Okay."

It occurred to me as I rested my head on the pillow that on the off chance those guys didn't pass out somewhere else in the station, they were going to eventually come in and sleep in the same room. Every time I would begin to give in to sleep, someone would open the door and flood the room with light, and I would jolt awake. While I lay there on the bed, I wondered who I would tell. Who would care? I was sure I would be told to forget about it because "they were drunk and didn't mean it." It was just one more bad memory in a fire house.

I always feared this moment would come. Once, someone had asked me about my firefighting and in a hushed voice they said "have any firefighters ever *touched* you?" The answer had always been no, of course not but I was honestly always expecting it. Firefighters had tried everything else to throw me out of their world, why wouldn't they try this?

I watched the digital numbers on the clock creep closer toward daylight. My body finally gave into sleep somewhere around dawn. Will woke me by throwing a pillow in my direction. I grabbed my backpack and followed him out of the bunkroom without looking back. The rest of the station was still asleep when we loaded into his car and headed north, back home. I no longer felt brave. I felt small, irrelevant, and damaged beyond repair. Feeling it was simply too much. Each time I remembered it was like experiencing it all over again. So I began to train myself how not to feel.

I also stayed silent. I protected my town from knowing that the firefighters who were willing and able to come and save them were just a theory. I protected Will and Evan from feeling like they had to fix everything for me. I protected my parents from seeing what was happening to their daughter. I knew that out of love they would make me stop and I just wasn't ready. I was always the protector. No one was there to protect me when I needed it.

Back at home I sat in the shower, trying to wash it all away. I felt too small to see. My knees were tucked under my chin. I fought the instinct to move as the scalding water burned my skin pink. More of me was washing away. I looked at the distorted image of myself in the faucet handle. I unclamped my hand from around my shin and noticed the way my fingertips had puckered. I watched steam rise slowly off the bathtub floor, like the fog rising off a wheat field. Disgust dripped from my pores. Disgrace mixed with the water and collected around the shower drain. In an attempt to retain my femininity, I had painted my toe nails pink. They were long since chipped and I watched the water droplets roll off them and away from me. I looked down at my bare skin and traced the veins coming from my heart. I thought that if I looked hard enough I could see why the love I used to feel was slipping away.

As Jim spoke, he leaned forward in his seat to get my attention.

I was slipping. I no longer had a firm grasp on my thoughts. Jim appeared when I needed an outlet to talk, some way to release and I needed that now more than ever before.

"What do you think Ali? Are you going to forgive them?"

I stared at him in response to his absurd question. My mind was still processing and forgiveness was nowhere on my radar. As I was about to answer no, Jim cut me off.

"Do you believe that every person is redeemable? Do you believe that everyone deserves to be forgiven? I do. I know it takes a lot of persistence to be free of hate, to forgive

completely. I think when we see that our anger does not change anything, that's when we can start to let it go. It does not reform these men for you to stay mad at them forever. It was never your job to change them. Forgiving them doesn't mean you have to forget. If not for them, forgive for yourself so that you can move away from your anger."

Jim leaned back, gesturing with his hands for emphasis.

"There will always be people in this world who don't understand you, don't understand the way that you do things. There will be some people who will see your goodness and try to take it. But all of the things that make you who you are, are qualities that cannot be lost or taken away. The world's ignorance does not change who you are. Don't let it change who you are. You are indestructible."

Rubbing my head, trying to erase images from my mind, I stated: "I don't want to talk about this."

"You have to."

"No, I don't. Get out of my head, please just leave me alone."

In the train seat, I curled into a ball. I turned my face away from Jim and stared out the window.

* * *

Later that month, tones dropped for a vehicle accident with injuries: motorcycle vs. bike with one head injury. Out of habit, I responded. Evan was in command of the call. As the rescue approached the scene, he told the driver to be careful because the patient was lying in the roadway. I jumped out of the rescue and began to move. There was a teenage boy lying in the road. A firefighter was already holding his neck still. Someone told me to get a backboard, so I retrieved one and placed it on the ground near the patient. I heard someone call him Christian. His hands were shaking. The other people were treating his possible injuries, so I tried to catch his eye. I felt calmness flow over me. Christian's arm was bleeding badly and he had a strip of bloody road rash across his forehead.

I rested my fingertips on Christian's wrist, a small show of comfort. Ricky's hand brushed mine as he moved to roughly pat Christian's skin, and I stopped for a moment. I was surprised to see him act in a caring way, this person who I had permanently placed in that category of people, the kind of person who only did unkind things. Ricky was comforting Christian the same way I would. A show of sincere sympathy from Ricky was not something I had ever expected to see.

Before the firefighters rolled him onto the backboard, I reached across and pulled up Christian's shirt to reveal a long, bleeding scrape on his back caused by his skin skidding across the pavement. The medics took note of this and readied more gauze pads for him. Christian's eyes were locked on mine. My face was right above his. Once he was secured on the stretcher, he began firing questions at me. What did his bike look like? What did his head look like? Was he bleeding? Was he going to die? I answered the best I could, avoiding the last question. Just before they boarded him into the ambulance, Christian started to cry. His neck was being held in position, so his face was toward the sky and the tears dripped down past his ear and onto my fingers. He was slipping into shock and I talked to him quietly. Into the ambulance he went, where the doors closed and he was gone.

After we got back to the station, I stepped out onto the ramp in front of the truck bay. I was forcing my mind to chronicle Christian's accident so I could remember the completeness I felt after helping him. The sun was setting behind the mountains that encircled my small piece of the world. I raised my arm to wave goodbye to Evan as I left the station. From his rearview mirror, a wooden cross dangled in the vanishing sunlight. The shadow of it swayed across Evan's face as he smiled at me. It was a reminder, a small sign that made me think maybe I wasn't alone.

That is a powerful, nearly indescribable feeling. I knew Christian was feeding off my energy because at the moment, he didn't have any. I would hold on to the feeling of his fingers gripping mine when I needed to remember why I loved firefighting. Yet my world was still far from peaceful.

When we were younger, my little sister and I would lie in bed at night, staring at the glow-in-the-dark stars stuck to our ceiling and I would tell her why things were the way they were: why elephants were gray and why weeping willows were so sad. I made up stories, giving reasons for things I didn't understand. I thought of this one night as I wrestled with sleep, staring at the same ceiling with no stars. I was no longer that naïve little thing who could explain away things she didn't understand. No matter how hard I thought about it, I still could not think of a reason for why I seemed to be causing such disruption in a world where I felt so called to be.

* * *

A moving train is never still, similar to the way a ship constantly rocks while at sea. Jim held the book firmly as the train swayed on the track like a pendulum. His strong hand moved over the page as he wrote.

"I can't believe what that place has become for me." Tears fell unnoticed down my face as I spoke. Jim stayed silent, his eyes still focused on what he was writing. I grew angry.

"And since you seem to know everything, tell me this. What is the point?! Because of those people at the fire house, I don't trust anyone anymore. I don't see how I ever will."

Jim hummed softly. It sounded like someone had plucked the low strings of a perfectly tuned guitar. He spoke calmly to alleviate my anger.

"You are focusing too much on the end result. We all want to know why we have to go through a certain experience and exactly how it will benefit us in the end. Just keep living. Before you know it, you will never be the person you were before. Sometimes I think that's the point, to be the person on the other side."

* * *

In the fall, I was at the abandoned training house with my fire company. The fire company was training on how to properly extinguish chimney fires. I was sitting on the front of the fire engine, trying to be invisible. My eyes were open but I was staring straight ahead, looking for something I couldn't quite see. My arms were crossed tightly across my chest, protecting me. I was forcing myself to think of happy things. I hummed a melody in my mind and began to feel a release. My hands loosened their grip on my arms. I was barely noticing all the people moving around me until someone stood right in front of my face and jolted me out of my happy place and into that destructive reality.

It was Patrick. "Get up. Let's go."

I squinted up at him. Rudely, I spat. "Let's go where?"

My heart involuntarily closed shut, my voice was thick with hatred. I stared back at him as other firefighters stopped to look. Feeling like I had nothing left to lose and no other way out, I made my way up the extension ladder leaning against the front of the house. My right arm was bent at a 90-degree angle and was slung through the rungs of a 16-foot roof ladder. Each step up made me wince, the side of the roof ladder was resting on my shoulder and the other side pressed into my hip. The ladder pressed into me so heavily I could almost feel the blood vessels breaking, the dark blood pooling beneath my skin.

Because of the degree of danger and the difficulty of the training, there were supposed to be three people on the roof at a time. When I got to the top, it was just me and another firefighter, who was literally frozen in place by his fear of heights. Glancing down at the cold ground beneath us, I could easily see it rushing up to meet my face, just like it had done when I fell off the roof simulator months before. I straddled the roof peak, facing the chimney. Looking down past the roof line, I could see the expressionless faces of about a dozen firefighters who were standing silent, staring up at me. There were two chiefs standing next to each other, apart from the rest of the group. I looked at them, not sure what kind of help I was looking for. One looked away and the other just stared blankly back at me.

Will came up the ladder and reached across the roof to hand me the chimney snuffer, which looks like a silver torpedo with holes in it. It was attached to a hose that snaked back to the ground and connected to the fire engine. Will smiled at me, but I ignored it. He went back to the ground. At a chimney fire, the snuffer is attached to a hose and then the firefighter lowers the snuffer down the chimney and in theory, the water pumps through the holes and extinguishes the fire. I knew that a firefighter was supposed to stand on the extension ladder and feed hose to the roof since gravity makes managing the hose difficult. So I wasn't surprised when I heard someone climbing up the ladder toward me. As I turned away from the chimney to reach down and grab the extra hose, I saw that it was him.

He saw my eyes open with surprise and then grow hard as my body flooded with exhausted anger. I watched helplessly as a sadistic, cruel smile spread across his face. I scrambled, quickly grabbing for the hose lying nearby. As soon as my hands had a grasp on it, I pulled. Patrick simply leaned forward, pinning the hose between his hip and the roof line, effectively halting my progress. I pulled again, but it was in vain. It was like a lion playing with his food. Most of the people on the ground could not see what Patrick was doing. All they saw was me pulling as hard as I possibly could and the hose not moving an inch. A tiny cry escaped my lips. Patrick's eyebrow rose as he saw his task of humiliating me accomplished. After what seemed like an eternity in this devil's tug of war, he finally grew tired of his game. With a smirk on his face, Patrick let up on the hose and disappeared beneath the roof line. With shaking hands I completed the evolution the best way I could, but when I made it back down to the ground I was beaten. Yanking off my heavy helmet, the dark hair that I no longer bothered to hide fell in front of my face like a shroud. With my eyes down, I walked wordlessly through the crowd that parted before me.

Undressing for bed later that night, I pulled up my shirt to expose a crescent moon shaped bruise curving around my hip bone. This time, I could see the evidence of the hurt my body was holding inside.

I was supposed to be learning and I was. Just not about fire fighting. I had plans to visit a college near Philadelphia that offered a degree program for firefighting. But I did not dare get my hopes up that it would be a good place for me. I felt like no place would be right for me.

* * *

Walking to my locker at the fire house one night, my foot connected with something plastic and I involuntarily kicked it across the truck bay. Reaching behind a fire truck tire, I pulled out a DVD case. It was porn. Irritably, I flung it back onto the floor. A few days earlier I had been "accidentally" sent porn through my fire company email and through multiple text messages on my cell phone. Shocking? Sure. Surprising? Not even a little bit.

They made me feel embarrassed for wanting to be successful as a firefighter. Even though I had absolutely nothing to be ashamed of, I started to consciously and unconsciously hide what I was a part of. I started to put my pager in the front pocket of my sweatshirt instead of clipping it to my jeans. I cut my hair short so it would be easier to conceal in my helmet. The small silver firefighting medallion that I used to wear so proudly as a necklace was now always tucked safely against my skin. I was so used to always being singled out and told I was "wrong" that I just wanted to blend in.

I began to talk less and less until the only conversation of substance that existed was between me and Jim. In reality, my only escape became music. It was the feeling of my drum sticks smacking into the drumhead that seemed to give me the greatest relief. I spent hours a day in the garage, pounding out my disappointment on the drums, breaking more drumsticks than I kept intact. I only stopped when my blistered and tired fingers began to bleed. I sat on my bed wrapping my finger in white medical tape when Jim interrupted.

He looked at me, sizing me up. "You know, I don't even really think this is about you."

I looked down at my hands, and was surprised not to see tape or blisters. Sighing, I dropped them into my lap.

"Who else do you see sitting here?"

Jim smiled. "Yes, you are having this experience in your life, but this isn't really about you. It's not personal. This is not happening because you, Ali Warren, are such a problem. It is more about what they think a woman's role is in society. It's because you won't let them silence you. These men have very different views than you do."

"Obviously."

"But it's not really about you, or even about the oppression of women."

"How's that?"

"It's about people who misidentify themselves as oppressors. We sometimes put ourselves in these boxes. We put up these walls and say to others, 'you aren't like me. I'm going to keep you out.' That's all they're doing."

"It's not an excuse."

"I'm not saying that is it. But listen. Sometimes we move around like we have no impact on each other, like we are living in this world alone. The world is so small, but it's all we know. All we have is what we have together. The more walls we can take down in ourselves the easier it is to coexist with others. When you put it all aside, it's remarkable how alike we all are."

I sat up tall, slightly confused. "So you're saying that I am like them?"

"I'm saying don't turn this into you vs. them. I'm saying that we are all on a path to discover who we are. But we are all in different places on the path. Some take different turns, get stuck in different places, some skip over certain parts entirely. Some get lost."

This made sense to me, but I was still hung up on the situation. "There are people that could be helping make this more bearable for me."

Jim nodded, understanding it all. "I know. Sometimes we close our eyes because we don't want to see something, because seeing it means we have to choose a side. But this is what I'm trying to tell you, sweetheart. What these people are doing is not personal to you, even though it feels that way."

He spoke with a more relaxed tone.

"It's all based on love, really. Like your love for this job. You have to learn to love them too. Love them. It's the only way to free yourself."

I nodded. "I'll try."

Jim leaned back and closed his eyes giving me time to let the conversation sink in.

I watched him. "I love you."

We are each other's keepers.

Chapter 7

War or Peace?

"A sailboat will last a very long time in the harbor but that is not what it was designed for."

Author Unknown

* * *

Car accidents are a different challenge for firefighters. We know that the injuries usually are not life threatening, and despite the fact that the patient is afraid, they probably won't die. We have seen it so many times before: the flashing lights, the twisted metal and broken glass, the blood. Because of that regularity, it is easy for firefighters to lose compassion. But not showing compassion is also a defense mechanism. We have so much more to protect ourselves against than just fire.

In the evening, the tones went off as I was getting undressed. I quickly put my shirt back on, inside out and backwards and rushed out the door. The dispatcher's ever-calm voice told me that the accident was just a block away from the fire house. On my way to the station I crossed over the intersection, looked to my left, and could make out the flashing lights of a police cruiser stopped in the middle of the street. It didn't take us long to arrive on scene, so I was still fumbling with my safety glasses and searching for the right size of rubber gloves when we pulled up. We screeched to a stop and I saw that there were two cars, a smaller four-door and an SUV. I jumped out and began to move. Pulling on the gloves, I walked over to the car with the most

111

damage. There was a teenage girl sitting in the front seat. Her face was wet but her eyes were clear, as if she had just stopped crying. A police officer was leaning against the door frame, keeping her company until the firefighters arrived.

He spoke calmly to me. "This is Vanessa." He gestured down.

She was looking up at me. Heavy traffic was stopped all around us, cars in all directions of the intersection. I knelt down next to Vanessa to look for her injuries. The cop walked back to his car, and most of the other firefighters were still standing near the rescue. I was on my own.

I saw that Vanessa had a cut behind her left ear and some glass gleamed in the skin over her right eye. Blood was slowly making its way down her face. Two firefighters appeared on either side of me, standing far enough away to let me work, but close enough to offer any help. One of them set the medical bag on the hood of the car and began handing me different sizes of gauze pads. He smiled at me. It was an "I will be your friend today because people are watching, but your enemy tomorrow" kind of smile. Rolling my eyes, I took the gauze from his hands. Another firefighter crawled into the seat behind Vanessa and held her head in place until the medics arrived.

"Hi." I tried to keep my voice light and I worked quickly to slow my adrenaline-fueled breathing. "My name's Ali. I'm with the fire department."

Vanessa looked at me, unsure and shaken. "I'm Vanessa. My head hurts."

"I bet it does. Here." I placed gauze onto the cut above her eye and held it there. "So. Can you tell me what day it is, Vanessa?"

"Saturday."

"Who is the president?"

"George Bush."

"And what's my name?"

"You're Ali. Ow." She winced as I applied pressure to the gash behind her ear.

"Sorry." I touched the hand that was sitting loosely in Vanessa's lap while my other hand held the gauze in place.

"Does anything else hurt? Your neck?"

"No, it's a little stiff though." The firefighter behind her adjusted his hands as her light hair fell over his fingers.

"Yeah, it's probably going to be really sore tomorrow. You took a pretty good hit. Do you remember everything from the accident until now? Did you black out at all?"

"Um, I remember it all."

There we were, two teenage girls, having a conversation like we weren't sitting in the middle of the road in Vanessa's busted-up car with her bloody face in my hands. The medics pulled onto the scene after we had been talking for just a few minutes and I explained to Vanessa that they would be moving her to a stretcher so she could go in the ambulance to the hospital. I moved out of the way so the medics had access to Vanessa. As the medics were preparing to move her out of the car seat and onto the stretcher, one of the medics had me come back in and hold

Vanessa's neck until she was in the laying-down position. As my fingers spread around Vanessa's ears and my hands cupped near her jaw bone, Vanessa looked up and I held her gaze for a few seconds. I just smiled down, as I was feeling the usual calm I felt when I knew someone was looking to me for reassurance and stability. All firefighters have these moments of quiet glory, when there is no speculation as to the effect one can have on another. The collar was placed around Vanessa's neck and she was wheeled to the waiting ambulance, then into the ambulance, and she was gone.

Sometimes when I let myself slip into the hole of doubt and darkness, I felt so far from my dreams. I was fighting for something I didn't actually know existed. At every fire house I had ever been in, I was stared at like a freak on display. Each time I felt that way, it got harder to pull myself out of it. I had to reach inside of myself and find something that was still good about me. Only then could I crawl out of the ditch of the depression I so often found myself in.

My mind continued to be my battlefield. That's where I fought. Sometimes I felt closer to beating the struggle going on inside, the murderous feeling of inadequacy. But every time I attempted something new, whether it was a fire skill or anything that required me to be something I might not be, I got a particular image in my head. I saw myself at sixteen, sitting in a chair with Chief Ray leaning over me. I heard him telling me in his roundabout way that I would never be good enough. I saw myself nodding like a bobble head, agreeing, wanting him to accept me. And then I went blank. It was like a broken record that played over and over in my mind, a movie that I couldn't seem to stop. Bad memories keep you in the past. They were making me fight for who I was and for who I wanted to be despite them.

* * *

One early winter morning, we were on our way back to the station after a fire in town had gone to a second alarm. It was after 3 a.m. and the gradual movement of the rescue was rocking me back to sleep. As we approached a stop light, the blinking yellow lights bled into my consciousness and I opened my eyes. Without moving my head, I glanced at the men sleeping all around me. With their eyes closed, I felt like I could study them instead of it always being the other way around. The three sitting next to me were asleep with their heads leaned back. The two across from me were slumped over in opposite directions. The man directly across from me had his head resting on the window that I was leaning against. I glanced down at our feet. Four feet in identical boots, grimy with the toes scuffed. From the neck down, we all looked the same. Our massive coats made us all appear to be heavy, our helmets balanced on our knees, our suspenders hung down at our sides. The only thing I was ever told was how different I was. What about all the things that made us the same?

* * *

It was time for me to try again for my Firefighter 1 certification. I had three skill stations to retake: hose line advancement, roof simulator, and water supply. But it was so much more than a test for me. It was the next step toward reaching these goals, the next step to getting away. If I passed this test and successfully received this certification, other fire departments would consider me to have at least the basic firefighter skills and they would consider me as a possible future member.

In the weeks before my redo, I had no one to help me train. I didn't really have anyone to help me figure out how to not fail again. I read books to learn technique, and watched the way my dad's hands gripped the axe as he demonstrated for me. I asked Sam, the assistant chief who took over for Ray, if my dad or mom could come down to the station and be there to supervise me so I could try to cut through the makeshift roof simulator behind the fire house. Sam had agreed, but when he was questioned by Patrick, he appeared to not remember the conversation. I was almost written up again. The threat was always there, a ghastly gift waiting if I ever made them too angry.

One day while I was training on the roof simulator behind the fire station, I lost it. I stumbled off the simulator and let the tears come. That was the piece of equipment I had fallen off a few months before and my shoulder still throbbed anytime I remembered. I leaned against the building next to the roof simulator, my gear pulled me to the ground. I hated that I was there, doing all of this alone.

Waiting for sleep that night, I found myself in the train seat. My legs jiggled with pent-up nervous energy. My left hand was curled into a fist and I pushed it against the ever-present headache in my skull bone between my eyebrows. I didn't bother to look up to see if Jim was there.

"I can't do this."

"How do you know that?"

I stared at Jim. How could he possibly think this was going to be okay?

"Are you kidding me? There is no freaking way…"

Matching my attitude without being mean, Jim smirked. "Oh, I see. You are still under the impression that this is supposed to be easy. Ali, just because life is challenging doesn't mean that there is something wrong with it."

Jim sighed, knowing that I was still struggling.

"Look at me."

My eyes rose to meet his.

"Everything you need exists in you completely. You don't have to go looking for it, or say some magic words to make it appear. It's there already. Listen to me when I tell you, you are enough."

I fell asleep peacefully. Jim's words were always exactly what I needed to hear at the moment. He was the buffer between me and the world.

The day arrived. The FF1 evaluator came out and I shook his hand. He was very nice, but I was not thinking about being friendly at the time. He asked me in what order I wanted to do the stations and my head was screaming "roof simulator!" but I couldn't get my mouth to say it. I could see my dad out of the corner of my eye mouthing "roof simulator." Eventually I spit out the words and we walked over to the simulator. My dad hugged me vigorously, and his arms gave me strength. He drove off to the other side of the academy grounds because I told him not to watch. So this was it. I found myself standing in front of the roof simulator with all the tools spread out in front of me. The evaluator had the skill sheet papers in his hands. He asked me if I was ready. I honestly couldn't get my mouth to work. Literally, I felt as if all my moments had been leading up to this one. It was so much more than just a test to pass, or just skill stations to get through.

I managed to nod. He read the instructions that they have to read to all FF1 candidates and asked if I had any questions. I had none. I knew what I had to do. With shaking hands I began. I grabbed the roof ladder and opened the hooks on the ground. I picked it up, slid it up on the roof simulator and set the hooks into the roof peak. With the ladder set, I moved to the pike pole which is a big long pole with a hook on the end. I placed my foot firmly on the first rung of the ladder and climbed up as I sounded the roof with the pike pole. I got to the top, placed the hook of the pole in the top rung of the ladder and climbed back down. Next: the chain saw. I test started the chain saw on the ground like we have to do; there is no use getting all the way up on the roof with a saw that doesn't start. I turned it off and hauled it up onto the roof, checking my balance every step of the way.

I visualized the hole I wanted to cut, and then restarted the chain saw. It started with one pull. With the roar of it in my ears, I stretched my body as far as it would stretch and cut the right side of the rectangular hole. I pulled back and cut the top side as well as the inspection cut. Done with the saw, it went back to the ground. I was getting closer. Next: the axe. I climbed back on up. I planted my feet firmly and imagined that they were super glued to the wood beneath me. I cleared my mind of everything except for making the cut. I put my hands close together, brought the axe up over my right shoulder and swung down with all the strength inside of me. The axe shattered through the wood, a clean cut. I exhaled. I finished the rest of the evolution, not hiding the smile on my face. I cut the final side with the axe, the side closest to me, which was the most physically challenging. I cleared the hole with the handle end of the tool and saw that all had gone according to plan. Then I brought all the tools down off the roof, and returned everything back to the position that I found it.

I turned to face the evaluator. He knew this was big for me. He smiled warmly. "Congratulations, firefighter."

As important as that was for me, I still had two more stations to complete. The water supply station was easy. It involved hooking up the correct-size hose to the correct inlet on the fire engine. I made it through that. There was one left.

My last and final skill was hose-line advancement up a ladder, in through a second story window, down the stairs to extinguish an imaginary basement fire. As I was doing this skill without a partner I didn't have to do as many steps. As we were walking over to the burn tower, I spotted my dad off at the other end of the academy, sitting in our blue minivan. I knew that the only thing keeping me from this victory and giving my dad a happy hug was this last skill. I did not care how much effort it took, I was going to pass this. Failing was not even an option anymore.

Off I went. The evaluator was outside the building so he could charge the line for me when I called for it. I carried the uncharged hose line properly up the ladder and in through the second floor window. I sounded the floor before stepping onto it and then made sure the hose was flaked out so it wouldn't kink up and delay the water. Then I ran into a small problem. Before I began the evolution, I put my face piece on, but I didn't have the air regulator in place, so no air was flowing into the mask. When I rounded the corner, saw the basement steps and went to call for water, I realized that I couldn't see. My face piece was completely fogged up, and since I never actually needed to hook the air regulator to the face piece, it never got cleared up. I could see out of the very bottom left corner of my mask and that was it. I got angry about this, but angry in the way that made me strong. I gritted my teeth and held the hose nozzle tight to my body. Nothing was going to stop me from passing, not even a fogged-over face piece.

I heard the evaluator tell me that he heard me call for water. I didn't even remember I was supposed to crawl backwards down the stairs until I was at the top of them looking down. So I turned around and went down the correct way, pulling the hose with me. My knees were killing me from pounding into each concrete step, but I was never more determined. Just seconds to go. In that moment, I thought clearly and surely that God was with me, that the presence was closer than the sunlight or the air I was breathing. That's it, nothing complex, just a simple thought. I made it to the bottom of the stairs and managed to see the orange cone that was my basement fire. I hit the orange cone with the correct stream of water and the evaluator told me to shut down the hose line.

He walked out of the building ahead of me and I was nearly stepping on his feet to get out, get my gear off and have him tell me that I passed. We got outside and I ripped off my helmet, flash hood, and face piece. The gloves fell to the ground. Again the evaluator smiled. "Congratulations."

I had done it.

We re-rolled the hose and put all the tools back on to the engine that we had been using. I tipped my head back slightly, hoping that the tears welling up in my eyes would spill back into my head. My dad rushed at me and picked me up off the ground with the force of his hug. It had been almost four months to the day since I fell off the roof simulator in my last attempt. The weight I had been carrying was slowly lifting off my shoulders like a hot air balloon rising off the ground.

* * *

It is surprising how quickly one can move while half asleep, adrenaline helps a good bit too. I pulled a sweatshirt on, pressed contacts on my eyes and suddenly I could see. As I ran through the house and made my way outside, I talked to myself to help me wake up.

"Don't run into the table, watch the dog, *why* is it sleeting?"

Sometimes there would be a little voice in my head that would pop up and say, *This is stupid. Go home, go back to sleep. Be normal.* But I would just laugh at that incredulous little voice because when your heart is speaking so loudly, you don't dare argue. We would sit in a row of pickup trucks at that intersection, our cars idling while we wiped sleep from our eyes. Like swimmers waiting for the gunshot to set us free, we would wait in caged anticipation for that green light. The station was in our sight line. We could see where we wanted to be, but we had to wait to get there.

* * *

Sleep did not come easily for me. I usually wrestled with thoughts until my mind and body were entirely exhausted. Even though there had been redemptive moments for me recently, they would soon be forgotten. When I fell into sleep, I knew I would probably be woken up by the tones. I was already wearing sweatpants and a sweatshirt and had sneakers next to the bed. Everyone had been talking about the possibility of accidents during the night because of the impending snow and ice storm. So when the tones pulled me from slumber right around 2 a.m., I wasn't surprised. Obligation rose with me.

It took me seconds to get from the bed to the bathroom. Ignoring the dark circles under my eyes I grabbed a bottle of contact solution. Blinking quickly, I tried to settle the contacts on my eyes and whispered that I was going on a call to my now-awake parents.

"Ali?" My mom whispered in an effort to not wake up my sister, who was sleeping in the room across the hall.

"What?" I was impatient.

My dad's voice was groggy and it reminded me that it was in fact the middle of the night. "Be careful."

I rushed outside and my shins collided with the car sitting in the driveway as the pavement was now a solid sheet of ice. I gasped as freezing cold air filled my lungs. I was completely awake when I heard the dispatcher's voice naming my fire company as the second-due engine company on a working building fire downtown. My hands gripped the steering wheel tighter as I heard firefighters already at the fire calling for more fire personnel to the scene.

The firefighters I found when I arrived at the station were not at all bleary-eyed—this was a big call and everyone knew it. We responded in the engine with five instead of six, which would make all the seats full. I assumed that I would be taking the position of hitting the hydrant when we got on scene. As we sped off through the night, I keyed up my headset and asked an assistant chief if he wanted to do the break (hook the hose from the hydrant to the engine) while I hit the hydrant.

A firefighter ripped off his headset, stuck his big finger in my face and yelled "You hit the hydrant! You hit the hydrant!"

I did not ask him, nor did I want his opinion, but he was far into his uncontrollable fanatical fire call mentality and there was no use arguing with him. The assistant chief calmly told me that he would connect the break for me. It was just below freezing and a little after 2 a.m.

We arrived in the alley, to the left and back of the building where the fire had originated. By listening to radio traffic we learned that the fire had spread to the neighboring exposures down the block. I was the first out of the engine and fell to the ground as soon as my feet landed. "Well that was graceful," I grunted as I found my footing.

Walking around to the back of the engine, I picked out the heavy hydrant bag and slung it over my shoulder. The heavy 5-inch metal hydrant adapters swung and hit me in the ribs. With my left hand, I pulled on the orange webbing that was looped up inside the hose in the hose bed. I yanked on it as hard as I could and began to run the short distance to the hydrant. The engine driver quickly realized that a police car was blocking us from laying the hose into the fire building. We could not park the engine any closer to the scene and could not get the hose closer to the fire. Some firefighters went off to find a hose line that was closer to the fire. At that moment, it didn't matter how fast I opened the hydrant, we could not advance the line off our engine anyway. Still, I wasted no time.

There was a yellow concrete cylinder in the ground next to the hydrant. It was leaning in the direction of the hydrant, as if a car had hit it and knocked it off balance. I knew I wouldn't be able to turn the hydrant wrench with that there. I kicked at it and it wiggled. With my gloved hand, I pushed snow away from the base and saw that some concrete was missing. I bent my knees, reached down, and pulled the entire thing out of the ground and laid it in the snow. I placed the hydrant wrench on top of the hydrant so it wouldn't be lost in the snow. Wanting to be certain that the hose did not kink when I charged it, I began to walk the length of it to make sure it was flaked out properly. Suddenly, the firefighter who had yelled at me in the engine came out of nowhere, barreling at me. He grabbed the wrench off the top of the hydrant and pushed, loosened the top and then threw the wrench back at me. I moved out of the way to avoid the heavy metal tool and was shocked at his complete abandonment of his job, but I had no time to ponder this as the police officer had moved his car and the engine driver was calling for water. I charged the hydrant and flooded the hose with water.

The crowd of drunken bar hoppers had gathered outside in the snow. They acted like the alcohol made them not feel the bitter cold of the night. They called out, mocking us and cheering when firefighters appeared out of the smoking fire building.

Another firefighter and I walked over to the staging to see where help was needed. Soon after we arrived, we were asked to advance a hose line into the back of one of the business buildings on the block. My partner and I had brought air packs over with us and had laid them in the snow. We picked them up, dusted them off and got ready to enter the fire building.

Once inside, the lack of visibility astonished me. It took me completely off guard. I turned around and could barely make out the patch of light that was my exit. More firefighters entered behind me. With all of our hands on the hose line we began to look for the fire. After just a few minutes inside, I felt my back start to vibrate. It was the quarter service alarm on the air pack going off, telling me that I was running out of air. That startled me; I had just entered the fire building and should have almost a full cylinder of air on my back. I suddenly realized that I had not checked the cylinder after I picked it up from the snow. I pictured the scowling faces of the men who had stared at me as I laid it there. Would one of them actually dare to let air out of the cylinder when they knew my life would depend on it?

Motioning to the firefighter, I hurried out of the building. Ripping off my face piece to breathe, I saw the faces of the other firefighters. They thought I had to come out because I was too scared. I heard the rumor floating through the frigid night air. It settled into the firefighters like snow resting on a flower petal. That firefighter told everyone I was too weak to open the hydrant so he had to do it for me. No one questioned it because that painted the picture they wanted to see.

After spending hours standing in the frozen streets, my fire company was placed available. Back home, I crawled back into bed smelling of smoke, asleep before I hit the pillow. As soon as my eyes closed, I was back there. I had the hose in my hands and I was advancing the line up the steps and into the fire building. I was concentrating on my breathing like I usually did, making sure that it was calm so I didn't waste my air supply. I was trying to find a way to the fire through the yellow-gray smoke. Then I took a breath and nothing happened, like there was no air in the world left for me to breathe. Dropping the hose, I grabbed at my mouth but found that my hands were thick with fire gloves and they hit the plastic of the face piece. I tried again, seeing my hands come at me but not being able to get to my skin. I screamed out. My voice was angry and loud in my head but there was no one around that cared to hear. The smoke pushed in from all directions.

I yelled at myself, "Why can't I breathe? Breathe! Breathe!"

I woke up to darkness weighing down on me, like the fog that sets down deep in the mossy crevices of the mountainside. Pushing the bed covers down the length of my body, I kicked them to the floor. I took a few breaths until it was steady, until my lungs were filled to capacity. Then I let the air out in one big whoosh, startling the silence in my bedroom. Focusing on just that, air, I tried to sleep. Just breathe.

* * *

It was wintertime. Snow sat heavy on the trees, the branches hung near the ground. I looked up at Will as he walked toward me. The smile that was on my face faded. His face was blank, expressionless, tired. His eyes rose to meet mine and I tensed up inside, knowing I was going to get hit.

I opened my mouth. "What." It was a flat statement, said with no emotion. I knew that I could not hold anymore in me, I needed whatever he was going to say not to be bad.

Will looked at me for a moment before answering, as he if wanted to give me a little more time of living without knowing this information. "They signed a petition against you." He spoke slowly, as if he was trying to spread out the hurt evenly so it wouldn't land too hard in one spot.

We had been through so much together; Will had helped me fight this. He had to fight his own battle by being associated with helping me fight mine.

Blindly I stared at him. "What does that mean?"

He sighed. "It means that when you come down to go on a call, they won't ride with you."

I laughed out loud in disbelief. "They can't do that. We won't get any of the trucks out if there is no one on them!"

Will rubbed his forehead. "No one is going to stop them."

Will was studying me, watching carefully for signs of a breakdown. There were no visible signs from the outside, but internally the war waging in me was about to end. Those firefighters were going to win by giving me no other choice but to leave. How could I be selfish enough to stay when my presence meant others wouldn't get help quickly?

My world became flat. My mind finally finished unraveling. Petition. They were writing down their hatred for me in black and white. My mind began to spin. If I continued to be a firefighter, people would no longer get the help they needed. It would be my fault. They would not get the help they needed because fire trucks would not respond to their emergencies because of me. Petition. With that disturbing news, my fragile and breaking mind was pushed off the cliff it had been teetering on.

"Are you okay?" Will asked. "Yeah." Lie.

"Are you sure?"

"Yes." Lie.

"Ali..."

"I'm fine." Liar.

Will fought to get my attention. He looked me square in the eye. "Ali. They will not get away with this."

Cynically, I smiled. "Yes they will." Truth.

My faith in mankind evaporated.

"Ali."

Jim's voice broke through the screaming in my head. I spoke to him slowly, but deliberately. I fought to stay in control.

"I cannot believe," I paused to gather myself, "that I fought for so long and now I have to give it up anyway." I placed hope in Jim's eyes, praying that my explanation was enough for him. So much in life is taken from what we don't say, from the silence, from the spaces between our words.

"I can't stay, Jim. People will stop getting help if I stay. I just don't want to give it up."

"You aren't giving it up! You are still a firefighter. They can't take that away because that is something no one can touch. You will find a fire house where you can survive without fighting every day. Remember what I told you about this not being personal?"

"It is, though!"

"No, it isn't. This is a very small battle in the war that people are fighting all over the world against injustices that you can't even imagine. I know that this seems like such a huge mess but how do you know this isn't getting you to where you were always meant to be?" I shook my head in disbelief. "I feel so lost."

Jim didn't seem worried. "Sometimes we have to lose ourselves to find who we really are."

I sighed heavily in response to his logic.

Out of desperation, I finally decided to break the silence. I told officials in my town about the petition, but they were not surprised. Their facial expressions didn't even change, not a raised eyebrow, no dropped jaw. When I finally summoned the courage to confide in a local police officer, he said, "Well, yeah." As if to say, "you stupid little *girl,* how could you not know that this is the way the world works?" I believed I was the only one who actually saw the injustice.

I hated what my name was to them. According to these men, I was this person who was a troublemaker, a waste of space, a slut, a whore, a home wrecker. According to them, I was a bad firefighter. I was the topic of their every conversation. I was what they laughed about, I was their punch line. I had done absolutely nothing to harm them. Every day I was friendly and I smiled when all I really wanted to do was punch them until they couldn't say my name anymore. I was an outsider. They still said disgusting things about my body while standing right in front of me. I knew I would never get used to that. This fact weighed heavily on me: this was the job my heart had chosen. There was nothing I could do about that and I didn't want it any other way. So I was going to have to deal with this type of work environment for the rest of my life.

Chapter 8

Something Beautiful

Just because something has never been doesn't mean it never will be. It is okay to be the first at something.

* * *

Tones went off for a building fire in town and my fire company's engine was second due. I responded, with the possibility of the petition sitting heavy in the back of my mind. I got dressed like always, and sat there in the engine. I watched firefighters arrive, notice me on the engine and take off their gear. Eventually we had enough firefighters to respond. The firefighters that were first due from another station never knew of it, they never found out why our engine was so incredibly late to respond. The fire company did its best to bury it all and hide me away. People in the town who had known me for my entire whole life would ask questions about my firefighting. It would have made things so much worse if the firefighters knew I was talking about them, so I was forced to lie in an attempt to save myself from future drama. It drove me crazy to see that everything was so covered up, that I lived in such a secret.

At the end of the year, the fire company chose new assistant chiefs for the following year. The people who were chosen were the masterminds behind the whole get-rid-of-Ali plan. Patrick was one of the new chiefs voted in.

Standing in the station one night, I laughed at one of the nice firefighters. He was dancing around the fire house in his fire gear, running into the lockers and the truck tires. I wasn't laughing out of amusement, but out of relief to know that there were still good people in the world that didn't want to cause me trouble or hurt others.

I loved sitting at home doing something random and hearing my pager go off, the monotony of the day interrupted again. I loved how my mind knew that it was my company's tones before the alert tone even beeped and the red light flashed. I loved how fast I could move, sweatshirt, shoes, keys. I loved how I didn't even remember the drive to the fire house afterward because my mind was preparing to fly into action the second I tore open the station door. I loved how fast I could go: emergency brake, car into park, keys out, seat belt off, into the station. I loved how my head would turn slightly to see which fire truck was turned on. To my locker. I loved how I would throw my car keys in, not even looking where they landed. Pants out, suspenders out, shoes off. Feet in, pants up, suspenders on. Coat over shoulder, grab helmet, turn, don't trip, now run. I loved how I would vault inside each fire truck, pick a seat and tag up. In the engine: on went the flash hood, air pack straps on, do it quickly but correctly, it could save your life. In the rescue: rubber gloves, extrication gloves, safety glasses. Sit still.

I loved how I would strain to hear the voices on the radio, to find out what we were flying down the road to. I loved how I could pick up key words over the wail of the sirens like "working fire" or "entrapment." I loved how I would strain to see past heads and air packs and dangling headsets to see cars moving out of our way because we were the fire department and we will rescue you in your emergency.

I loved how I would rest my hands on my knees, calm from the outside, while on the inside, I was bustling with energy and adrenaline, ready to go. When we were approaching the scene, I loved how my hand went to the seat belt release so I could do whatever needed to be done. I loved how I would size up a fire scene, taking in everything.

I loved how I proved them wrong. I loved how I did that job with a passion I did not know I had in me. I did not plan on it. I found it in myself, by accident. It was given to me, a beautiful gift. Now it was my job not to lose it. I would remind myself of these things that I loved when it almost became too much. Of all the things that the firefighters said about me, what embarrassed me the most was that some people thought that I was sleeping with some of the firefighters. It hurt me deeply that people thought I was like that. They thought I was just like some of those other women. Everything I had tried to separate myself from now tried to define me.

Mostly, I wanted all of this turmoil to mean something.

But when I put it all aside, the fire house was still magical to me. That fire house was like a cave, harboring sleeping giants that could rumble to life at any given moment. I loved how the station just sat there, dark and silent until the alert tone sounded. No matter the time of day or night, people came running from all over town as that building kicked into life. Even when it was nighttime and everything was sleeping, I would fling open the door and find people all disheveled and sleepy, trying to collect themselves so we could run off together to help.

Calls came in and I didn't go on all of them because of the boycott. My heart was breaking but I told myself it was necessary. I needed to survive that fire house and keep alive the dream they were trying to steal. I never faltered from my convictions. I now believed in the goodness of firefighting more than I ever had. I loved it fiercely, and it was bonded to me the way a tattoo is set in skin.

* * *

It was the time of year when winter and spring were fighting for dominance. At the time, winter was still winning. I was standing at the front window in my living room, watching the snow tumble furiously down out of the sky. I was anticipating an accident, and could not deny myself. I was already wearing two sweatshirts and shoes with the laces loosened so they could be slipped off easily. I heard the pager frequency open and I turned, as if responding to the sound of my name being called. I also turned away from the promise I had made to myself to not get involved with that fire house again. The tones dropped for a multi-vehicle accident with multiple injuries and I was off, like I had been doing it my entire life.

I made the left turn into the fire house parking lot and felt the brakes on the car lock up. I skidded on the snow and narrowly missed the stone wall at the entrance to the lot. Leaning forward with my chest touching the steering wheel, I struggled to make out the station in front of me. When I opened the car door, the frozen snow stung my face. I squinted against the cold and could barely make out the other firefighters who were running through the parking lot.

Their pagers were pressed to their ears as the snow muted all sounds. They jumped over ice patches that lay like a quilt on the front ramp. Two red trucks loudly rumbled to life, one after the other. We all hopped in, wiping moisture off of our faces. We pulled the thick coat collars up over our ears and the thick gloves over our hands. I asked a fellow firefighter to hand me the box of rubber gloves and when he ignored me, Ricky handed me an extra pair he carried. It was a gesture I wouldn't mistake for kindness. Anything that could be mistaken as a considerate act was only to get me to lower my guard so I could be abused again.

The scene was a battlefield and the casualties were cars. They were strewn everywhere, SUVs and tractor-trailers and small two doors with smashed-in hoods and passenger-door panels. We firefighters all grabbed tools as we scrambled to get out of the rescue and reach all of those possibly injured. I grabbed a flat-headed axe. I ran down the hill in between the two lanes of stopped traffic. I came to the first car; it had a dented hood. I knocked, and then realized I couldn't be heard over the howling wind. I tore open the door.

The passengers were stunned and sat huddled together in the back seat. They stared at me with wide eyes.

"Hi," I said breathlessly. "Is anybody hurt in here?"

A girl who was sitting in the front passenger seat had a thin cut on her chin from striking the dashboard. As I got near to her to inspect it, to look for glass inside the blood, we looked at each other. I felt it again. The feeling when I knew that whatever that girl needed, I would give.

* * *

I continued to respond to fire calls, just a few every couple of weeks. I picked calls where there was no life at risk. The petition made the fire company's response time longer, but the surprise quickly wore off for me. It was not out of the ordinary for me to watch a firefighter walk into the station, notice me, and then walk right back out. Thankfully there were a few people who realized the situation and made sure to respond so we could keep things moving. That fire house was not about firefighting anymore, it hadn't been for a long time. In the beginning, before everything turned dark, everyone still recognized there was a common goal. This concept had slipped away, I felt it every time I walked in there. It was now about childish games. It was beyond a personality conflict. It had become a life safety issue for me. If I went into a fire with one of the men who did not care about my safety, I may not come out of it. To say that I was going to take a break from firefighting absolutely broke my heart. I had no other place to do it. What other choice did I have but to stay?

* * *

Just a few days after the accident, a call came in the middle of the day for a gas leak inside a house that was under construction. I quickly calculated the people who I thought would be most likely to respond. I figured my biggest adversaries would be at work so I went to the station. It was just Ray, a driver for the engine, and me. No one else seemed to be coming, so we responded with three.

The gas company had arrived before us and shut off the leak but we were needed to go into the house and check for dangerous gas levels. The driver of the engine walked over to talk to a member of the construction company.

It was just Ray and me standing there silently, looking at each other. Ray couldn't avoid working with me without making a scene in front of the crowd of construction workers standing near us. The gas meter was in his hand and I noticed his face piece hanging at his side. I took a breath.

"We really should pack up." I looked up at him. "We don't know how much gas is in there." I glanced into his eyes, expecting to find them empty as usual. Usually there was a certain sadness that inhabited them, and I had simply grown accustomed to it.

But today, it was different in his eyes. They were clear and I could see my Chief Ray again. He was right there, looking down at me. His eyes were full of grief and guilt. There was compassion erupting in his long-dormant soul, I could see it.

It was like we both had words ready to say but no one wanted to speak first. I couldn't find enough courage to open my mouth so I took the gas meter out of his hand and turned. With just enough movement to keep forward momentum, I walked in the direction of the newly built house.

As Ray walked behind me, I wished I could ask what he thought of me now. I had done it; I had accomplished everything he had told me to look forward to in the beginning. I wanted to ask him, *"Are you proud of me?"* Then anger came. *"You saw me in a sling and you didn't even care to ask. Why don't you care what happens to me anymore?"*

Ray and I walked through the dark and empty house. Cardboard lay across the new floors, muddy with the workers' footprints. Darkness hung like a curtain. I was tempted to open my mouth every time the clunk of Ray's rubber boots stopped, but the words never came. As we walked deeper into the house, I felt less and less afraid of him. I wanted so badly to say something, something other than the standard non-response to show that I was not afraid. *"Ray, we can go back. I'm not mad, we can start over."* But the words were never said. We stepped outside and the warmth in his eyes was gone. Ray walked toward the engine and away from me.

* * *

A call came in for a vehicle accident with entrapment and fire. It had the potential to be big from the get go, so I decided to ride. My hatred for them pulsed as my heart beat faster and I hated myself for that feeling. I arrived at the station with two people already in the engine. My mind quickly sped up. There was someone trapped in a car that was on fire and they needed that fire out to have a chance to survive. If I got on the engine, I knew that they would both get off, further prolonging help. So I decided to take extra long getting dressed so I would not make the engine unable to respond because of my presence.

In the end, the call was nothing, no injured passenger, no fire, just steam coming from the smashed engine compartment. I knew how bad that would have been, to have someone trapped in a burning car with no fire truck coming. There would have been no explanation. But the fire company lucked out again, and the secret remained hidden for another day.

I went home, angry and exhausted. My family was cleaning up from dinner as I walked in the door and when they saw the usual look on my face, they didn't even have to ask what had happened. They knew that it was the same as it always was, disappointing.

My sister looked up at me and sighed. My mom put a hand on my shoulder.

"Ali, you really shouldn't let them upset you anymore. Are you really still surprised by what they do?"

Moving out from under her touch, I walked toward my room. "I'm not upset because of what they do. But because of what they do, I know what my choice has to be."

Some pressure was lifted since I didn't force myself to go on all calls. But I felt the presence of these demoralizing events every moment of every day. Like weights sitting on my shoulders, it pulled me down. Every day I was trying to discover a new way to stop feeling so disheartened and to heal permanently. I found a large piece of butcher paper and began to write. After about an hour, the paper was black with the names and events that I could not reconcile with. I taped the paper to the back of my bedroom door. It went from the top and hung down to the bottom. With smudges of Sharpie on my arm, I sat on my bedroom floor and stared. It was an interesting feeling to look at it all there in one place, as if those events could be crumpled up and simply thrown away. My eyes scanned that paper until darkness fell and I could no longer see across the room. It hung there for months. It was there in the morning when I was getting ready for school, when I sat on my bed to talk with my sister, and when I shut off the light to go to sleep.

Chapter 9

City

"Do not let your fire go out spark by irreplaceable spark, in the hopeless swaps of the approximate, the not-quite, the not-yet and the not-at-all. Do not let the hero in your soul perish, in lonely frustration for the life you deserved, but have never been able to reach. Check your road and the nature of your battle. The world you desire can be won. It exists, it is real, it is possible, it is yours."

Ayn Rand, *Atlas Shrugged*

* * *

Every person who comes into this world must make the decision as to what type of person they want to be. Establishing yourself once is not enough. It's an ongoing, constant effort to separate yourself from who you feel that you are, and from who you want to become. Going on a life-affirming trip to San Francisco was my step toward making those sides of myself one.

Opportunity came to me at a time when I needed it more than anything. My mom was sitting with me in the orthodontist's office when a magazine caught her eye. The theme of the magazine was women in leadership positions and one of the lead articles included the chief of the San Francisco Fire Department, a woman. When my mom first showed me the picture, I thought to myself that the chief's shoulders looked strong, like they could take a lot.

"You should call her or email her or something." That night my parents stood in front of me as I avoided their gaze.

"That's stupid."

"Why is it stupid?"

"Because she is not going to talk to me! Come on, Mom. It's the *chief of the San Francisco Fire Department!*"

"Ali, it could help. It's important to find other women firefighters to talk to, to see if women ever become accepted and how they dealt with any bias against them. Maybe you can relate to them and they can help you get through this."

They were begging me to take this step.

"Al," my dad said. "The only thing you know for sure is that nothing will happen if you don't try. Come on. Give it a shot."

"I'll think about it."

* * *

After a heartfelt email to the chief and a phone call from her, the visit to the West Coast was set. The San Francisco Fire Chief told me that if I could get myself there, the department would take care of the rest. I was going to spend an entire week with the paid men and women from the San Francisco Fire Department.

My days were now spent in happy anticipation, all leading up to the moment when I got on that plane bound for the West Coast. I did not sleep the night before. I lay in bed and felt myself breathe a little easier. My dad woke me in the morning and we traveled to the airport. The sun had not risen yet, and my parents and I sat in the quiet airport terminal. After a hug goodbye, I stepped on the plane and took a huge step toward my future. The plane rose steadily up into the air and as we broke through the thin layer of clouds settling on top of the mountain, I was greeted with a sight I had never seen before. Sunrise had finally broken and sherbet purple clouds spread out across the sky. I knew the trip was blessed from the beginning.

In San Francisco, California, I was greeted at the airport by a female firefighter, Laura. Her long blonde hair was softly gathered into a ponytail behind her head and the uniform she wore was pressed and clean. We drove through the peaceful looking city to the fire department headquarters. As I walked through the building to meet the chief, faces popped up from office cubicles.

"Hey Ali!" A firefighter I had never met before slapped me on the back as another shook my hand. "Welcome! So glad you could come!"

A man with a thick mustache stepped out of his office and greeted me. "Hey kid, how was the flight?"

In the moments before I met the chief, I excused myself to the bathroom. I stared at myself in the mirror, at my brown eyes, at the cheeks that had so often seen tears. Taking a breath, I smoothed my shirt and ran my fingers through my hair.

Back in the hallway outside of the chief's office, Laura smiled down at me excitedly. "You ready, girl?"

Laura opened the door to the chief's office and I walked in. The chief greeted me with open arms, literally, and enveloped me with a hug that seemed to push some strength back in. "So glad you made it, Ali. What do you think so far?"

I smiled comfortably under the gaze of the people in the office. "This city is beautiful."

Laura, the chief, and I sat down at the large wooden conference table in the chief's office. I looked around in awe at the dozens of awards, certificates, pictures and books that decorated her office. A San Francisco Fire Department coffee mug sat on the table waiting for me. In it was a rolled-up station t-shirt and an official fire department pen. As the women sat down around me, I touched the mug with steady fingers like I was making sure everything was real.

Laura re-did her pony tail. "So, you made it."

I sat down in the chair they pulled out for me. "Yes, I did. Thank you. I'm so glad to be here."

The chief unbuttoned the top button on her dark blue jacket and relaxed in her chair. "So. Tell me again, what made you find us?"

I cleared my throat as the women looked at me intently. "Well, basically I've been kind of having a rough time at my fire house for the past few years."

Laura looked over her dark-rimmed glasses at me. "In Pennsylvania, right?"

"Yup, right in the middle of the state. Um...my mom saw an article about you in a magazine. I am just at the point now where I can't deal with it alone anymore. I have been fighting for this for what feels like forever. I just need to know that what I'm fighting for exists."

The two firefighters smiled at each other. Laura touched my hand. "Oh hun, sure it exists. Just look at us! I understand that they have not been kind to you."

I quietly scoffed at the understatement. "No, ma'am."

Laura glanced at the chief. "Been there."

I looked between them and took a hopeful breath. "Yeah?"

"Oh yeah. Imagine how hard it was for us like twenty years ago. Don't you worry about them any more. You are here with us now."

The chief nodded. "And soon, really soon Ali, you are going to see that there is so much more than the hard stuff, more than the things that make you question your choice. All there will be is your love for this." I forced myself to suppress happy tears, as I felt the safest I had in a long time. I knew that I would never settle for less than that.

I was to stay in the beautiful, vacant top floor of a firefighter's four-story Victorian house. I stood in the living room, looking out over the city as dusk fell. Tears fell down my cheeks as I held my cell phone up to my ear.

"This is most beautiful thing I have ever seen." Those were the only words I could muster to explain it to my mom.

I heard the smile in her voice. "You made it, babe."

The next morning a different firefighter, Amber, picked me up to take me to one of the stations for the day. Amber walked up to me and again, I was greeted with a hug. We drove through the early-morning light and got a cup of coffee before driving to the station. I felt like I was talking to my future, to the person I could be if I did not quit.

Around lunchtime at the station that I was visiting, it was quiet. I was hoping they would have some calls so I would able to ride along and observe everything. A few firefighters were running on the treadmill, one was watching TV and stitching a hole in her gear, a few were doing paperwork. I walked into the kitchen, where a firefighter was making lunch. He greeted me with a smile.

I washed my hands at the sink. "Hey."

"Hi Ali, how are ya?"

"Good, good. Need any help?"

He handed me a head of lettuce and I began to carefully tear the pieces off and wash them. A few moments later, the tones sounded throughout the station. The dispatcher's voice boomed loudly, telling the firefighters to respond to a local barber shop for an unconscious male. I dropped the lettuce in the sink and ran with the firefighter to the truck bay, where he pulled on his gear as I stepped up into the fire truck. Amber was the officer of that shift and I watched her sit up front confidently, pulling her rubber gloves on. I smiled at her strength. The driver of the engine flipped on the siren and pulled on the air horn as they rolled out of the station. His massive biceps flexed as he turned the steering wheel sharply to avoid the cars parked carelessly on the street. The call wasn't much. The man had gotten lightheaded and fallen to the ground. The paramedics loaded him into the ambulance and he was gone.

As I walked out of the station, Amber called after me. "Remember Ali, all that we are we owe."

The firefighters in the San Francisco Fire Department welcomed me into their family simply because I love the same job they do. They did not need to know anything more. I shook dozens of hands, returned an endless amount of smiles and walked into so many fire houses in one week I almost lost count. I have all of their smiles saved in my memory and when I need to, I pull them out. Their existence gives me peace.

On my last night in the city, I was visiting the fire station which housed the fire boats. One of the firefighters was giving me a tour and I followed him outside, looking down at my camera. The door creaked open and I looked up. Without thinking, I raised my camera and snapped. The San Francisco Bay spread coolly out before me. The Bay Bridge stood out proudly overhead. Twin fire boats flanked the station door. Bright purple geraniums spilled out of their pots, unable to be contained. The bay lapped quietly at the dock. In the city where hope lives, the world is eternally peaceful. I had never felt so free. Firefighters filtered out of the station behind me, laughing, eating, and slapping each other on the back. I felt no hesitation. Together, we all climbed onto one of the fire boats and slowly backed away from the dock. I watched the city as we slowly moved across the water.

Two firefighters joined me at the bow of the boat, asking what I thought of the city from a boat's point of view and about the fire service as a whole. I could not believe I was there, in that moment. I turned to look at this firefighter's gentle face, at eyes that held no hatred for me.

"Firefighting...it's been hard for me." I went with the easiest answer.

Playfully nudging me in the shoulder, he reassured me. "You'll be okay."

"I know."

With the slight spray of the San Francisco Bay on my face, I decided that there is no such thing as irrevocable damage. Finding the missing piece makes the entire puzzle whole. That place, that city, and those people helped heal me.

* * *

Armed with the scrapbook of the recent trip, I marched into my fire station as if I belonged there. Evan was so excited to see me taking steps to get out of our fire house and he wanted to see the pictures I had taken. I was dressed in black shorts and a plain white tank top. My freshly tanned summer skin was in stark contrast with the harsh lights of the truck bay. I ignored the firefighters that bluntly stared at me, at the skin they had never been permitted to see. After talking to Evan, I smiled at them as I walked out the door. My smile said, "Look. I am healing, in spite of you."

* * *

Upon graduation from high school, I decided to attend a college that offered a degree in fire science. While a college degree is not required to be a firefighter, it shows employers that one is serious about the job and is a plus when it comes to promotions. On my last day home before I left for college, tones went off for a vehicle accident with one injury. At first, out of habit, I did not make any move to go. But I quickly calculated the likelihood of the biggest bullies being available for the call, and then realized how much I wanted to go and grabbed some socks. I got into the station through the already-open bay doors and saw that the rescue was already idling. The crew in the rescue was the usual day responders, with the exception of one guy who I vaguely recognized. The accident was just down the road, so we didn't really have a lot of time to get ready. I did, however, have on full turnouts and rubber gloves. It was the end of August and I had begun to sweat before the rescue stopped moving. As the firefighters were getting out, Sam called over his shoulder, "Hey Al, you got patient care, right?"

There was an older man sitting in a chair that someone had placed beneath him. I made my way over to him. This poor man was bleeding heavily from his face and as I saw this, my instincts took over. There was a bystander kneeling next to him with his hand on the injured man's shoulder. That was nice for me to see, someone being decent to a stranger. When I got to him and was standing there looking down at them, the helpful bystander backed away, saying, "It's okay. Help is here now."

I introduced myself to the patient, Owen. He claimed that he was fine, even though the amount of blood draining from his nose seemed to be coming out faster and faster. Sam handed me the medical bag. I opened a stack of gauze and began wiping the blood away from Owen's mouth. I asked him if he could breathe all right and he responded with a nasally "yes."

Then the firefighter who I vaguely recognized appeared next to me with a red biohazard bag. He laid it open next to me and knelt down. I was really surprised for a few seconds, that a firefighter would be nice to me on a fire call. Then Owen sniffed and I snapped back to the task at hand. The unfamiliar firefighter moved the medical bag closer to himself and started handing me the various supplies he thought I might need.

I was asking Owen constantly if he was okay, if anything else hurt, if he could still breathe okay. His nose had three different bends in it and each had its own cuts and bruises fully formed. We had just used up all the gauze in both medical bags when Owen started to say he couldn't breathe. I stuck a wad of gauze under his nose and told him to blow out. I was not prepared for the force at which he did. The gauze was blown out of the way and my face and arms were sprayed with little droplets of blood. I froze in the position I was kneeling and watched the blood spread like a flower blooming on my coat sleeve. I could not do anything about it because we now had even more blood to clean up. The firefighter next to me began to scramble to find more gauze. Sam hurried over and handed us a roll of paper towels, which was the only thing we had left.

We had a good system going. The firefighter next to me would get a paper towel, pour water on it, pass it across Owen's legs, and hand it to me. I would wipe blood and throw it in the biohazard bag. The ambulance finally arrived and we went through the well-rehearsed handoff. I helped Owen stand and lay down onto the stretcher. My gloves were slick with blood.

I walked over to the rescue and told Sam that I got blood on my face. Sam took a look, found antiseptic wipes and began to wipe it away. Then the firefighter who had been helping me came over and helped me take off my coat. He stood slightly behind me, and held out his arms. He sprayed it down with the bleach that all fire trucks carry. While Sam was wiping my face clean, I looked at him carefully. I saw the way his eyes scanned over my face, looking carefully for anything that could contaminate me. I decided to believe that he had done everything he could to fix all the problems at our fire house. Sam had done all he could, it just wasn't enough.

After the call, my dad and I went downtown to our favorite pizza place. I was standing in line waiting to order when I saw a recruitment poster for the fire department that my company so often ran calls with. Staring back at me was the firefighter who had just helped me on the call. I did not know what fire department he was from at the time of the call, so I was nice to him, like I usually was to people I didn't know. If I had realized that he was from that fire house, I would have been rude and standoffish. I would have assumed that he disliked me like everyone else and I would have been mean right back. He must have known who I was and what people said about me, but he was nice anyway. He didn't have to help me, but he did.

That is the last fire call I ever went on with my local fire company. I think of them, the firefighters still in my hometown, still in that mindset. Myths about the trouble-making Ali Warren will continue to haunt that place as long as the firefighters who fought with me remain. Any attempt to change this would be in vain as their minds have long since been made up about me.

* * *

It is the smell that would bring it all back to me. If I walked into that fire house right now, that's what would make it seem real again. It would hit me as soon as I walked in the door, before I even turned on the lights. Sweat. Rubber. Diesel fuel. Chewing tobacco. Wet hose. There is another scent there, nearly indistinguishable. It is fear.

Fear is everywhere. It is pushed into the backs of the fire truck tires, smudged across the toes of the rubber boots. Fear is placed high on top of the ladders and folded deep into the hose beds. Fear of change. Fear of growth. Fear of something unexplainable. But it's not my fear anymore.

That fire house is a place where fear fits like a straight jacket, where hate is worn like a winter coat, heavy and suffocating. It is a place where distrust is something that can be seen, it is the absence of light in their eyes.

* * *

"I don't know, Jim. I don't know why I can't let go of him."

"Him, who? Jared?"

"No. Ray."

"That's because you trusted him the most. He promised your safety, not only to you, but to your parents."

"I want to let him go."

Jim spoke wisely. "We work so hard to fit people perfectly into our lives only to find that we do not control when they come or go. If you do have to let someone go, you should try your best to do it out of love, not spite. It's okay. You can let him go now."

Once again, the thoughts I tried to keep from myself seeped into my subconscious as I slept. They played out like a movie in my mind. In reality, Ray stood a head taller than me. But in this dream, we stood eye to eye, toe to toe.

"I was sixteen! I didn't know that people like you existed. Why? Where did it start? In what moment did you decide to stop fighting for me?"

I was pounding on his chest, like I was playing a giant drum. Ray did not fight back, or try to shield himself from the blows. He just looked back at me and listened. After I had exhausted my anger, I gently fell to the floor. I realized it was the cool concrete of the fire house's truck bay and I laid my head on it. Finally defeated, I whispered, "I can't hate you anymore."

Ray knelt down next to me, his sneakers squeaking slightly as his legs bent. My eyes rose to meet his. He brushed hair away from my face. It was a gesture that brought tears to my eyes.

"Then don't. Let me go." It was simple coming from him.

I could see the gasoline stains on the floor. The gear hung in the lockers, courageous and clean. It was then that I realized the smell was gone. The fear of that place was gone. When I looked up, Ray was too.

When people say something is impossible,
what they really mean is that it's improbable.
It's completely possible, just unlikely.
Many things are improbable.
Nothing is impossible.

Chapter 10

Law of Love

"The very least you can do in your life is figure out what you hope for. And the most you can do is live inside that hope. Not admire it from a distance, but live right in it, under its roof."

Barbara Kingsolver, *Animal Dreams*

* * *

In college majoring in fire science, my motivation never wavered or changed. Firefighting was still the only thing I saw myself doing in my life. I was taught by teachers with decades of firefighting experience and they were thrilled to share with me. Sitting in one fire class late that fall, I noticed another fire student looking at me. I stared back habitually, testing him. He held my gaze. And then he smiled. It was a perfectly normal smile. It only lasted a second, but it made all the difference. It's the little things that mean the world to me.

True or not, it seems that the longer something goes without happening, the less likely it is that it will happen. It seemed almost impossible to me that I would ever find a fire house where I fit, a place where I could safely live out my dreams. It had been so very long since I was able to trust. But I was putting myself back into the job. I still believed.

The love of firefighting was with me the way a silhouette accompanies a soul. I could stop chasing after the dream, but it would always be there. I constantly wondered if it would be different for me the next time around. There was going to be that first time when I stepped into a fire house again. I couldn't help but wonder if it would be different.

But because of all the events that occurred in those few years of my young life, to me every person had two sides. There was the side that was usually the most dominant and that was how the person acted most of the time. But everyone always had another side, like an alter ego. I used to think that everyone I encountered would eventually show that evil alter ego and do things to try to hurt me. And I may or may not see it coming, most times I would not. Sometimes I could not separate the past from the present and I couldn't make the distinction that those hurtful people were not a part of my life anymore. I slowly started to realize that not everyone was out to get me.

* * *

On a wintery night when I was home from college, there was an accident, a car versus a charter bus. Right off the bat it was a huge call because of the potential for many victims. I got my scanner and began listening to the police reports that began pouring in. The passenger of the car was trapped with the dashboard pushed up against her chest. I was worried for her because I knew the probability of incompetent people coming to save her was very high. I heard the usual voices come over the radio. Their voices were filled with their personalities, strong and stubborn. I was flooded with emotion. I remembered running around that station with them, back before things had turned. No matter what, that station was where I began and it will hold a special place in my heart forever.

Away at college, I sat in class early one Saturday morning with a cup of hot chocolate balanced on my knee. A fire investigator was there to present to the class and his arson dog was going to do a demonstration on locating accelerants. The investigator was telling the class how he only let his dog work for a few minutes in the summer because as soon as dogs start to sweat, they open their mouths and can't sniff accelerants as efficiently. Turning his head to look directly at me, the only girl in the class, he smirked. "Well, she is a woman," referring to his dog. "Her mouth should be shut anyway."

I stared back at him, as my eyebrows rose slightly to show my unsurprised amusement. It's funny to me now, instead of offensive. It has to be because if I took time to see how dominant that type of thinking is in this world, I wouldn't be able to continue.

When I am asked what I do and say that I am a firefighter, the majority of people look right to my body. They don't even try to be discreet about it. Then they say, either with their eyes or their mouths, that "they don't really see me as the firefighting type." I know what numbers say about my chance of succeeding in this profession, and the likelihood of success gets smaller the higher up in rank I want to go. I know that the numbers say I am too small and too light, that my arms and legs aren't big enough. It's not that I don't hear the things they say. I just repeatedly remind myself not to listen to what the world is telling me. I choose to believe that my strength comes from an inexhaustible source that cannot be seen.

My perspective on the world was changed forever. I learned that you can be staring something right in the face and not see it for what it really is. The firefighters from my first fire station seemed like monsters wearing angel masks. I know how you can feel isolated in a room full of people. I know how staggering it can be when no one sees you, when you feel completely invisible. I feel that way a lot. But to become visible in the world that I choose to live in, I would have to be the one to put on the mask and become someone I wasn't, am not now, and never will be. So I choose to remain invisible. There will always be girls who are willing to do everything with their bodies to get what they want, anything from a pencil to a promotion. As long as they exist, I won't. So I choose invisibility over becoming someone I am not. I choose invisibility over becoming so visible, that I am all that they see.

My perspective was also changed in regard to love. I understand now what it is like to willingly give your life for something out of love, to be okay with the fact that one might have to give his or her life for another. I love this job. I love that this will never change.

I felt like nothing I did mattered anymore. Not fully healed, I did not join a fire company while I was at college. For two years I didn't run a single fire call. It seemed like an eternity, considering I never planned on stopping. Before, my life affected more than just me. Now I just sat in class and wrote papers on fire strategy and tactics, pre-emergency planning and the safest type of construction for house building. I got 100 percents on tests and didn't care. I listened to my fellow classmates talk about fires they went on and I felt like a piece of me was missing. Before, at any moment, my life could be wonderfully interrupted and seconds would be passed in a blur of red and adrenaline. Now, odd things like the high-pitched rumble of anything diesel fueled or the smell of wet pavement reminded me of the life I no longer had.

My dad learned about a professional female firefighter from a nearby city. I was eager to meet her and to have lunch. I needed to talk to someone who would understand.

A few weeks later, I sat at this woman's kitchen table. We stared at each other as we took turns speaking. We shared experiences no one else could imagine.

Sophia said, "After all this time, I still feel like I have been able to maintain my status as a woman, as a lady. I have never had to give that up. I am still me."

It was the answer to a question I hadn't asked, but an answer I needed to hear more than anything. I agreed to visit Sophia's fire department. I decided that it's all there will be, my love of this.

The night before, I found Jim in my dreams.

"I'm nervous."

"It's not going to happen again. You're not going to lose yourself like that again. There is a Law of Love that governs this world. This law applies to everything that exists, from the tenacity of a bird learning to fly, to the radiance of a sunbeam, to the warmth of a smile on an innocent face. It is

present in all of us completely, as if there were no others for it to be shared with. It's going to be different simply because the acts of a few do not define the rest. Your past does not define your future, so you can't look back. You have to learn from yourself and begin again, starting now."

Thunder boomed around 4 a.m. and I was awake. I hesitated in my slumber and waited for it. That usual nervous, acidic I-could-very-possibly-throw-up feeling was there, but only as a memory. What I felt on that summer morning was just leftover fear. I met Sophia and we drove together to her fire house. I was about to take a giant step back in to the world of firefighting. When we arrived, my heart sped up as I strained my neck to look at the building in its entirety. An American flag stood proud but faded as it fought against the rain. Sophia opened the station door and strode right in, like she belonged there.

I followed, but stopped to marvel at the trucks. They sat there strong, silent, and waiting.

The firefighters came in from all around the station. They all shook my hand and looked at me while I spoke. They looked at my face and not other parts of my body. We stood there in a circle, the common way to carry on a conversation in a fire house, steaming cups of coffee in hand. They made the circle wider so I could join them. I did not feel isolated or embarrassed while explaining to them how badly I wanted to be successful as a firefighter. There were no smirks, no downward glances at my body. In those moments, it did not escape me that I could have missed this chance if I had not kept up the fight. I kept fighting, and standing there with those firefighters was my reward.

There are some basic rules to follow when visiting another fire department. At meal times, sit down at the table last. One could very easily sit in someone else's unofficial assigned seat. Don't be the first to take food, or the last to take anything. When the meal is over, don't just stand up and leave. Put things back in the refrigerator, into the dishwasher, offer to sweep the floor.

The conversation over breakfast was light. Some of the firefighters were remodeling their houses, one firefighter's wife was expecting a baby. I felt so safe in knowing that at any second, the ordinary could be interrupted by the extraordinary.

Chauffeured around the city by the chief for that shift, I visited all four fire stations in the department. The chief drove me around and I felt comfortable with him, like I was driving around with my grandfather. My hands relaxed in my lap. The overcast sky softened the city's edges. The chief spoke about his love for the job, a love that mirrored mine. At each station, I sat at the kitchen table surrounded by firefighters. We talked about seemingly impossible technical rescues, terrifying apartment fires, and a love for the job that only firefighters can understand. They answered my questions and asked some of their own.

I smiled to myself while overhearing the way firefighters give each other directions. It's not by street names or well-known landmarks, but by locations of past fire calls. "It's down the street from where that semi rolled. You know, in the neighborhood where we had that two alarm last year."

As the end of the shift neared, the rookie firefighter was told to change the flag on the flag pole. He was instructed to take the truck's ladder up and I was asked to join him. We heard it start to rain again before we felt it. It was a drenching rain that fell and soaked us through in seconds. As it fell, it cleansed me. I turned my head toward the sky and laughed in defiance. Closing my eyes, I threw my head back and let the rain beat down. The other firefighter in the bucket with me was cursing and laughing as he messed with the buttons and we quickly descended back to the ground. Firefighters from inside the station came out and stood under the roof overhang to watch us scramble back down to the ground.

I stood in the truck bay, dripping water on the floor. I wiped wet hair out of my eyes and shook my arm to drip water on the shoes of the amused onlookers. One firefighter walked to his car and returned with a faded fire department shirt. It was three sizes too big and the fire department's name was slightly faded, but it was the best gift I could have been given. He handed it to me and pointed me in the direction of the women's bathroom.

I opened the door and stopped to turn on the light. I expected to find the room full of storage boxes like women's bathrooms in fire houses usually are. I flicked on the light and instead, there was a clean bathroom, shower on one end and a stall on the other. A towel with flowers hung on a towel rack. There were newly constructed shelves on the floor next to the sink, which held towels and soap that smelled like roses. A mini plastic zebra-striped hair dryer lay plugged in next to the sink.

Before, I had lived with the belief that in order to do this job, I would have to give up big parts of myself. My happy personality, my drive to succeed, and my determination were all things I thought I would simply have to check at the station door. I believed that no matter how pure my intentions, I would always be perceived as a monster. But in one shining moment, with one zebra-striped hair dryer, I realized: I didn't have to hide what I am.

<u>You</u> create your path.

Chapter 11

Final Destination

"There is no passion to be found by playing small – in settling for a life that is less than the one you are capable of living."

Nelson Mandella

* * *

Eventually, I quit my fire company. I stood on Sam's front porch, waiting for him to answer my knock. I looked down at the pager, charger, and mess of wires that were clutched to my chest. I knew I needed to heal, and in order to do that, I had to step away from that fire house. By returning those company-issued items, I knew that my absence would become official. I would no longer know when calls would come in. I would hear the sirens and wonder what was going on just like everyone else. Sam opened his front door, confused surprise spread across his face.

"Hi, Sam." I did not wait for his response. "Here. I don't need these anymore." Before he could protest, I passed the weight of our fire company into Sam's arms.

It had never been declared over. We've never said to each other, "It's done, it is finished. We can move on." So those events linger, more in some lives than in others. But it had a piece of all of us, we are forever changed. It's never been declared over because no one had ever admitted defeat. In my mind, the battle was done. I left that fire house with a simple close of the door, as quietly as I had arrived.

No pat on the back, no handshake, no "Hey, I know stuff got messed up here, but you did good, kid." Not one word. I wish that they could release it and live their lives free of hate. I wish they could stop hearing echoes of the past. I want them to be free from it. I really want that for them.

We shared these experiences together, they are the characters in my story. It is strange to me that their world seems to be unchanged when everything in mine is different. I drive past the fire house now as an outsider, as if I never even had a place there. It was Evan who remembered how deeply affected I was. More than a year after I told Sam I quit, after I had done most of my healing, Evan cared enough to clean out my belongings from the locker at the fire house. He returned them to me, passing them from his hands to mine like a precious gift.

* * *

Jim and I have talked a lot in the time since, more than ever before. One day as I stood in my bedroom, I heard a fire truck siren echo down the street. I asked Jim a question.

"I just want to know when it started. What was the moment when everything started to change? I keep racking my brain, trying to think of the memory but it's just not there.

Jim leaned back in his chair. He rubbed his forehead, searching for the right words to explain it all. His eyes grew thoughtful and he sighed deeply.

"Stop spending energy trying to pinpoint the exact time it all started. You can't. There is no conversation to be

remembered, no hidden answer to be found. You didn't miss the cataclysmic event; it never happened. Your presence just added fuel to the fire that was already burning. One day your eyes were opened up to it all. One day you were a kid and the next an adult, the effects are irreversible."

"I am going to be a firefighter for the rest of my life."

Jim smiled broadly. "I know."

"But in order to do that, I have to move forward from this. Forever. No more sadness for what happened, no more disappointment, no more doubts."

"Remember it like this. Those people taught you things about yourself you never would have learned otherwise. But if you never learn how to let go of this story, if you keep carrying it, how can you ever really live?" Jim placed his glasses back in the glasses case. His book sat in the seat next to him. He reached out to me and held my hand affectionately. He was surprisingly gentle for a man of his size. Jim's strength poured into me and filled the cracks that had formed in my soul. Jim spoke with authority.

"That's the trick to really living," he said emotionally. "To wake up each morning holding on to nothing negative from the day before. Life is not meant to be some giant burden passed from person to person, just transferring the load. This story was never meant to become a burden to you. Don't take the heaviness of it and carry it in yourself."

I smiled at Jim. "You know what?"

He smiled back. "What's that?"

I pondered for a moment before answering, "I think I'm close to forgiving them."

"How do you know?"

"Because these days I can see them for who they really are; people who can't hurt me, people who can't be hurt. They are blessed, courageous and making their way too."

"Then why are you crying?"

I hadn't realized that I was. "Because I just realized that I'm not going to carry this any longer."

Jim could not let me go without making sure I understood. He leaned forward out of his chair; his knees almost touched the train car floor. Jim looked past my tears and told me the thing I needed to hear the most.

"This was not your fault." I met his eyes and found there was truth living in them.

With relief, I began to cry harder. I didn't try to hold back the tears; I just blinked between them. Jim's face remained clear.

I questioned him, not sure what I was asking for. "Jim?"

"I'm here. I've always been here."

Jim handed me the book he still carried. The wrinkles in his face were soft crevices that mapped out the emotions of his life. Fishing a pen out of his pocket, he offered both to me. "Write it down."

I took the book carefully. I was feeling a particular strength, like I was wearing a protective armor that could not be seen. The book felt heavier than I expected, as if the emotion that the pages held increased its weight. The book did not appear to be old, it was just that the pages had been flipped so many times. I didn't realize that it was Jim's meticulous handwriting that filled the pages, telling my story.

I flipped through the book and saw that some of the handwritten words had bled. I grazed the words with my thumb and realized they had been smudged by tears shed. I flipped through the pages to the back, where there were only a few blank ones left. Holding the pen over the blank page, I didn't have to think very long before it all came pouring out of me.

Before, in a moment of bitterness, I had wondered if this would hurt less if more people shared the pain; if it wasn't such a secret. Now I see that this story is not about anger. It is about what happens after. I have seen the bad in people. I know how your heart can be rubbed raw after hurting over the same thing for so long. You have to keep looking for the good. It is out there, I promise.

Life is funny. It has a way of presenting us with the perfect moments to become exactly who we want to be. And it doesn't count against us if that opportunity comes twenty times before we recognize it and take it. It doesn't matter how long it takes us to get to where we want to be, just as long as we get there.

We achieve our dreams step by step, one step at a time. Sometimes that step is a big one. But most times, it is just waking up each morning with your dream still intact. It isn't easy, but it is worth it. Decide what you stand for and what you don't. Figure out what you want from life, even if it is as simple as not having an inconsequential one. Define yourself, instead of letting outside forces do it for you.

There is just life. There is no fair or unfair, nothing deserved or undeserved. And who are we to say what is good or bad when we don't have the whole picture? We don't have to have the whole picture. We have to have faith.

Do it. Do whatever makes you feel. Always do the things you think you can't do. Trust in the power that rules the universe, keep walking when the road is long, dare to be fiercely optimistic, and above all, believe in yourself and the power of your dreams.

There is just life. Don't be afraid to live it. Dream big.

Jim looked at the birds flying effortlessly outside the window as I cried, the last pieces of the story dripped from the corners of my eyes.

"We all write our own endings."

* * *

"Holding on to what is gone won't heal it."
—HANSON, *One More*

Acknowledgements

Thank you to those who helped me along in this journey.

To Chief Joanne Hayes-White, Mindy Talmadge, Nicol Juratovac, and all the members of the San Francisco Fire Department, Colleen Dunkelberger and Battalion Chief Herb Berger and all the members of the Harrisburg Bureau of Fire—your existence gives me peace.

To Jodi Picoult, Christopher McCandless aka Alexander Supertramp, and Henry David Thoreau—true explorers of life.

To Linda Dinardo, Jessie Barth, Betty Jane Dittmar, and Fujiko Signs for sharing the LOVE. Thank you for showing me how to allow myself to write this story and supporting me every single step of the way.

To my fourth grade teacher Mr. Rockower for introducing me to the wondrous world of storytelling.

To my enormous extended family. I cherish you. Thank you for loving me, for listening, for yellow pieces of torn cloth and for Facebook statuses becoming bookmarks.

To all the early readers, for your patience and belief and for dreaming the Big Dream with me.

To those special few who were there in the beginning. Thank you for fighting for what was right, not for what was easy.